MINNESOTA SPORTS TRIVIA

MINNESOTA SPORTS TRIVIA

Joel Rippel
and
J. Alexander Poulton

2011 by OverTime Books
First printed in 2011 10 9 8 7 6 5 4 3 2 1
Printed in Canada

All rights reserved. No part of this work covered by the copyrights hereon may be reproduced or used in any form or by any means—graphic, electronic or mechanical—without the prior written permission of the publisher, except for reviewers, who may quote brief passages. Any request for photocopying, recording, taping or storage on information retrieval systems of any part of this work shall be directed in writing to the publisher.

The Publisher: OverTime Books is an imprint of Éditions de la Montagne Verte

Library and Archives Canada Cataloguing in Publication

Rippel, Joel A., 1956–
          Minnesota sports trivia / Joel Rippel, J. Alexander Poulton.

ISBN 978-1-897277-62-1

          1. Sports—Minnesota—Miscellanea. I. Poulton, J. Alexander (Jay Alexander), 1977– II. Title.

GV584.M65R55 2011   796.09776   C2010-907613-3

Project Director: J. Alexander Poulton
Editor: Michelle Nichol
Proofreader: Wendy Pirk
Cover Images: Hubert H. Humphrey Metrodome: © 2010 Thinkstock; Target Field: © 2010 resedabear/Randy Stern; track sprinter: © Jupiterimages; hunter: © Photos.com; speed skater: © iStockphoto.com/corepics; lacrosse stick: © Hemera Technologies; golfer: © iStockphoto.com/Sergey Kashkin; football: © Toddtaulman | Dreamstime.com; baseball glove: © Bobbiholmes | Dreamstime.com; boxing gloves: © Zedcor Wholly Owned; all other images: © Photos.com

We acknowledge the financial support of the Government of Canada through the Book Publishing Industry Development Program (BPIDP) for our publishing activities.

 Canadian Heritage   Patrimoine canadien

PC: 1

Table of Contents

Introduction 8

Chapter 1:
Purple Pride 10

Chapter 2:
The Twins at Bat 45

Chapter 3:
The State of Hockey 81

Chapter 4:
On the Court 108

Chapter 5:
On Campus 133

Chapter 6:
Potpourri 168

Chapter 7:
Stadium Debates 185

Chapter 8:
Let's Not Forget 191

Chapter 9:
Minnesota Hall of Fame 201

Notes on Sources 205

Dedication

To Justin, Kelly, Ben and Sarah.

– Joel Rippel

To Helen Love

– J. Alexander Poulton

Acknowledgments

I would like to thank J. Alexander Poulton for giving me the opportunity to work on this project.

– *Joel Rippel*

Introduction

In March 1976, Minnesota politicians were debating the construction of a new stadium for the Minnesota Twins and the Minnesota Vikings. Many people were predicting that without a new home, the Twins and the Vikings would leave the state.

In its coverage of the debate, a Minneapolis newspaper quoted U.S. Senator Hubert Humphrey as telling the Minnesota House Democratic-Farmer-Labor Party Caucus that "great sports events are good for this community and are the best way to make Minnesota known to the rest of the country. Without professional sports, the Twin Cities would be just a cold Omaha. Don't miss the chance to give this state the opportunity to move forward."

A year later, a bill authorizing a new stadium was passed. The stadium—the Hubert H. Humphrey Metrodome—opened in 1982 and has provided Minnesota sports fans with many great memories.

But, with no disrespect meant to Senator Humphrey, long before the Twins and the Vikings arrived in the state—the 2010 seasons were the 50th in Minnesota for each franchise—Minnesota already held a unique place in American sports history.

Included in Minnesota's rich and diverse sports history are the Little Brown Jug, Bronko Nagurski, Bruce Smith, Patty Berg, George Mikan and Eveleth, the cradle of American hockey.

This book is a celebration of those legends and more.

Chapter One

Purple Pride

Minnesota's First Football Team

It wasn't the Vikings who first conquered the hearts of Minnesota football fans when they appeared in the National Football League (NFL) in 1961, but the Minneapolis Marines, who played throughout the Twin Cities from 1905 to 1924. Playing in several semi-pro leagues, Minnesota's first football club was composed mostly of working-class young men from the city. Most likely, none of the men had ever played organized football before and simply joined for the fun of the game.

It took a few years for the team to make a name for itself, but soon the Marines were at the top of their semi-pro league, winning the city championship in 1910. They continued to have success in their local semi-pro leagues throughout the decade, but in 1918 the team was forced to shut down operations because of the influenza pandemic that swept the globe that year. When the team was allowed to open its gates once again to the public, the Marines' owners had discovered that most of the players had signed more lucrative contracts with a rival team. It was decided that to keep the club afloat and to bring fans back to the team, the Marines would join the fledgling American Professional Football Association (later renamed the National Football League) in 1921.

The ploy to join the new league failed when the Marines posted a 4–11–2 record from 1921 through 1923. After finishing the 1924 season with a miserable 0–6 record, the team folded operations. They were welcomed back into the NFL family in 1929, this time as the Minneapolis Red Jackets. But, after a series of home games were rained out and attendance plummeted, the Red Jackets folded operations in 1930, and it would not be until 1961 that the state of Minnesota would return to professional football.

Viking Invasion

After having gone decades without a professional football team in their city, five businessmen from Minnesota—Bill Boyer, H.P. Skoglund, Max Winter, Ole Haugsrud and Bernie Ridder—got together and made their pitch to the American Football League (AFL) to start up a new team. In August 1959, the AFL (rival to the NFL, with which they would merge in 1970) awarded the five businessmen their franchise, but just five months later, in January 1960, the men forfeited their membership over financial issues and joined the rival NFL. With their future secure, the five owners set about building their team from the ground up. Bert Rose was hired on as the team's general manager, and the process of cobbling together a new franchise began.

Coming from his job as the director of public relations with the Los Angeles Rams, Rose knew a thing or two about marketing to an audience, and when the question of naming the new team came up, he was the first to suggest "Vikings" to the board of directors. Rose selected the name because it spoke to the Scandinavian tradition in the northern Midwest and also because the image of a Viking was one that represented aggression and a win-at-all-cost attitude.

Once named, the Vikings marketing machine kicked into full force, and by the time the club was ready to open the season at Metropolitan Stadium, they had sold close to 26,000 season tickets for the 40,800 seat stadium. In their first regular-season home game, played on September 17, 1961, the Vikings took on a very tough Chicago Bears team.

Before a packed Metropolitan Stadium, the Vikings surprised fans and sports pundits with an upset 37–13 victory over the Bears. The team was led by fresh-faced rookie quarterback Fran Tarkenton, who completed 17 of 23 passes for 250 yards and four touchdowns. Despite the incredible start, the reality of being an expansion team hit hard when the team lost seven straight games and ended the season with a 3–11 record. Still, the fans remained loyal to their new club, and after the club's first difficult steps, the fans were rewarded with some of the most exciting football in the league.

Sense of Direction

From 1961 to 1979, defensive end Jim Marshall faithfully served on the Viking line, helping the club to the 1969 NFL championship and earning two pro bowl selections in '68 and '69. He was one of the toughest defensive ends at the time and a bane to all opposing quarterbacks, but if there were one skill missing from his repertoire, it would have been his sense of direction. On October 25, 1964, he completed a play that to this day has to be one of the most embarrassing moments in professional sports history.

Defending against the San Francisco 49ers, Marshall recovered a fumble and, in the confusion, began to run toward his end zone. He ran 66 yards, unimpeded by any 49ers, into his own end. Thinking he had just scored a touchdown, Marshall threw the ball into the stands and raised his arms in celebration. But that celebration quickly turned to embarrassment when one of his opponents caught up to him and thanked him for the two-point safety. Marshall simply hung his head and walked off the field. A few days after the incident, he received a letter from Roy Riegels, who famously ran the wrong way in a 1929 Rose Bowl game, which said, "Welcome to the club." Marshall would go on to bigger and better things, but that one mistake still haunts his career.

Fran Tarkenton: NFL Career

Fran Tarkenton joined the Vikings in their inaugural season after being selected in the third round of the 1961 NFL draft. The 21-year-old quarterback showed so much promise that he was thrown immediately into service in the franchise's first game. He triumphantly announced his and the Vikings' arrival into professional football by leading the team to a 37–13 victory over the Chicago Bears. In that game, he passed for 250 yards and four touchdowns, making him the only player in NFL history to pass for four touchdowns in his first game.

From 1961 to 1966, Tarkenton was the Vikings' number one quarterback and was one of the major forces that gave the team their early identity. Despite the team's growing pains, Tarkenton could always be relied upon to provide some excitement on the field, as he often liked to run with the ball in the backfield. This wandering habit earned him nicknames like "The Mad Scrambler," "Frantic Fran" and "Scramblin' Fran" and also raised the ire of his head coaches. Under the leadership of Tarkenton, the Vikings were able to remove themselves from the basement of the league, but they could not make their way to the championship.

To capitalize on Tarkenton's tradability, he was shipped off to the New York Giants in 1967. From 1967 to 1971, he again helped another team out of the basement of the league but could not finish with a championship.

In 1972, Tarkenton was traded back to the Vikings and enjoyed some of his most successful years with the club. In 1973 and 1974, he led the Vikings through two excellent seasons and all the way to the Super Bowl, but once more, he could not deliver on the championship. Nearing the end of his career, Tarkenton still had the ability in 1976 to take the Vikings through another successful season and into the Super Bowl, but again he walked away without the title.

Sports historians have tended to be unkind in the treatment of his career because of his inability to bring a championship to the Vikings after three chances in the Super Bowl. Despite that fact, his career numbers speak to him being one of the greatest in NFL history. He is currently fifth on the all-time list of wins by a starting quarterback with 124 regular-season wins. His habit of carrying the ball racked up some 3674 rushing yards and 32 touchdowns. His 47,003 career passing yards put him in sixth place all-time and his 342 passing touchdowns are in fourth place in NFL history behind Brett Favre, Dan Marino and Peyton Manning. He retired from Vikings service in 1978.

Fran Tarkenton: Businessman

Even while he played for the Vikings, it was clear that Fran Tarkenton was more than just a football player. His guest-host spot on *Saturday Night Live* in January 1977 showed that he had a certain flair in front of the camera. After retiring from the game, he appeared on the television show *That's Incredible* and worked as a part-time commentator on *Monday Night Football*.

In 1969, he entered into the literary market when he published a book entitled *Broken Patterns: The Education of a Quarterback* that chronicled the entire 1969 regular season with the New York Giants. As his interests turned to the world of personal and business success, he penned two self-help motivational books: *Playing to Win* in 1984 and *How to Motivate People: The Team Strategy for Success* in 1986. His ability in front of the camera and passion for self-improvement led to an infomercial deal selling the famous self-help guidebook *Think and Grow Rich*.

Tarkenton would use his tools of motivation and success in business in the mid-1980s in helping to set up his own software company. The company was an instant success and made Tarkenton millions of dollars in profits. But, looking for a slower pace to life, he sold the business in 1994 to the Sterling Software Company for an undisclosed amount. Since then, he has kept busy promoting various products from self-help guru Anthony Robbins and opened up a financial consulting firm in 2003.

Brett is Back, then Gone, then Back, then... Arghhhhh

The saga begins in the not-so-distant past in the lovely town of Green Bay, WI, when a star veteran of the Green Bay Packers (a name which still makes me giggle childishly) decided to end his career and bow out of the professional limelight. It was a decision the fans of the Green Bay Packers did not want to hear but accepted for all the glorious years of service he had given them. Brett Favre was the face of the Packers for so many years and in 2006, when he made the decision to retire, he was applauded in rival stadiums as a respectful farewell and even gave a tearful interview after the final game of the season.

But, wait! After much back and forth throughout the off-season and intense media speculation, Favre made the miraculous announcement that he would return for the 2007 season. The questions around his status remained as he played through the season and helped the Packers get into the playoffs, although they ultimately fell to the eventual Super Bowl Champion, the New York Giants. It was a brilliant run that season for the veteran, but backup quarterback Aaron Rodgers was itching to take over and become the face of the new Packers. Again after much speculation in the press, Favre officially announced his retirement on March 4, 2008.

"I know I can play, but I don't think I want to. And that's really what it comes down to," Favre announced to the world.

Off to New York

There it was, as clear as day. Brett Favre would retire from professional football after valiantly leading his team on a push into the playoffs, although ultimately failing. He would walk out with his head held high.

Wait a second. Just four months later, it was reported by ESPN writer Chris Mortensen that Favre was quoted as saying he had the "itch" to return to football. However, after falling out with management over the repeated retirements that he felt he was pushed into, Favre decided to look for employment elsewhere.

On August 7, 2008, the Packers traded him to the New York Jets, but New York was an unkind and unhappy place for Favre and the team. His 2008 season was one of his worst in recent memory, and he was plagued by a nagging shoulder injury that slowed down his famous right trigger arm. At the end of the season, he informed the media once again that he was retiring from football. It was time to say goodbye to football; with the nagging injury issues he did not think he could perform at the level he expected.

Then he was back again. Surprise! After undergoing surgery for the damaged muscles and tendons in his arm, Favre found that his recovery had progressed faster than expected and a return to playing form might not be out of the question. Before the start of the 2009 season, it was announced that Brett Favre was once again un-retiring from the league to join the Minnesota Vikings.

Favre Puts On the Horns

Favre announced his intentions to join the Vikings on June 15, 2009, but Mr. Decisive himself decided on July 28, 2009, that he had changed his mind and would remain retired. Sure enough, Packers fans were secretly smiling because Favre was now doing to their rivals what he had done to them. But, as football fans have come to realize, the word of Brett Favre's retirement is never set in stone, and a couple weeks later, he officially signed on with the Vikings to start the 2009 season as their number one quarterback.

While some Packer fans prayed for Favre to falter, the graying veteran put in one of the best seasons of his career, surpassing several personal records he had set in his glory days as a younger player in Green Bay. In the course of the season, Favre became the first quarterback since the NFL's expansion in 2002 to register a win over all 32 franchises.

That final 32nd win was probably the most memorable game of his career. On October 5, 2009, Brett Favre jogged out of the tunnel of Lambeau Field in Green Bay wearing a Vikings jersey. He had defeated all teams but the one he had played with for so many years, and his appearance on the field was immediately followed by a wild chorus of boos and choice words from his former fans. Despite the game being played up by the media as a chance for revenge, Favre did not enjoy playing the role of the bad guy on the same field that had brought him so much glory.

"Packer fans cheer for the Packers first," he said.

As much as he tried to remain indifferent about any meaning behind the game, Favre ran onto that field with a little extra energy in his step, and his teammates were there to cover his back. He completed 17 of 28 passes while his defense sacked his old understudy Aaron Rodgers six times. The Vikings won the game 38–26 at Lambeau Field, and Favre ran off the field pumping his fists to an odd chorus of boos and cheers.

That game, however, was just the start of Favre's amazing season. After winning the NFC North Division, the Vikings looked like a team that might surprise with a spot in the Super Bowl. After dispensing of the Cowboys in the opening round, Favre and the Vikings traveled to New Orleans to play the Saints. The Vikings pushed on the offense but five turnovers led to several New Orleans gains. Regulation ended tied and moved into overtime where the Saints knocked in a 40-yard field goal for the win. Favre was devastated by the loss and although he considered another year with the Vikings, he faced the prospect of another surgery, this time on his knee, that might keep him from ever playing again. So, while he never announced his retirement, the off-season led to more speculation about his future.

"It was very tough, obviously. I could make a case for both—playing, not playing. All I could think was that I was so close to getting these guys (Vikings) to the Super Bowl," said Favre at a press conference.

So, Brett Favre has once again returned to action with the Minnesota Vikings for his 20th season in the NFL. The Vikings faithful are now lovingly attached to their veteran quarterback after the 2009 flirtation with the Super Bowl and expect great things from him. As for the future, Favre prefers a mystery.... Stay tuned.

The Gjallarhorn

In ancient Norse mythology, the gatekeeper god Heimdallr used the Gjallarhorn—a loud, Norse horn—to announce the coming of the final battle that would see the destruction of the world and its eventual rebirth. Its powerful sound bellowed across the land and the realm of the gods as a signal for the warriors to prepare for the ultimate war. It is this instrument and its warrior's call to action that Vikings fans have adopted and brought into their home stadium. It can very clearly be heard over the roar of the stadium after the Vikings make a significant play, get an important down or score a touchdown. Making the image of a Norse god battlefield more realistic, many fans show up to the game wearing the famous "Helga hats," purple hats with white horns and two blonde tassels said to mimic the helmets worn by ancient Viking warriors. To add to the godly war-like atmosphere, cannons fire off a flash of smoke whenever the home team scores a touchdown.

The Hail Mary

The Minnesota Vikings of the mid-1970s were a tough team to beat. They had the impenetrable defensive that became known as the "Purple People Eaters" and the mobile quarterbacking of legend Fran Tarkenton. Following the 1975 season, the Vikes were considered the ones to beat in the playoffs after going 12–2. Going into the NFC Divisional playoff against the Cowboys was not going to be easy, but if the

Vikings played their game the way they had all year, then things would come out in their favor.

The Vikings got the opening touchdowns in the second quarter, but Cowboy quarterback Roger Staubach managed to get his team back in the game with a touchdown of their own in the third to tie the game. Tarkenton gave the Vikings another touchdown in the fourth quarter, but all the Cowboys could muster was a three-point field goal. With the score 14–10 and the clock ticking away, it looked as though the Vikings had wrapped up the game and were ready to move on.

With one minute and 51 seconds left in the game and with the Cowboys on their own 15-yard line, it didn't look like Staubach could get his team up the field in time. Then, in one of those moments that leave those watching with their jaws on the floor, Staubach managed a nine-play drive that put him in the middle of the field with 24 seconds left on the clock. He called the play to his teammates, lined up in the shotgun formation, took the snap, faked, then turned to his right and threw a long desperation pass to wide receiver Drew Pearson, who had his own problems under tight coverage from Vikings cornerback Nate Wright. In a moment of divine intervention, Wright fell to the ground and Pearson, just barely catching the ball against his hip, simply walked across the goal line. The Cowboys converted on the extra point and the seconds ran out on the Vikings' playoff hopes once again. It was one of the most heartbreaking losses for Vikings fans to remember.

Following the touchdown, Viking safety Paul Krause complained to the field judge that an interference penalty should have been called on Pearson for impeding Wright. Krause might have mistaken an orange thrown onto the field by a spectator after the play to be the referee's penalty flag. As Vikings defensive tackle Alan Page took up the argument with the field judge, more debris began to fall down from the stands and one inebriated fan launched a whiskey bottle at the referee, resulting in a gash on the referee's forehead and rendering him unconscious. The Vikings had no chance to make it to the other end in the few seconds that remained and slunk off the field with their heads held low.

It was only in the post-game interview when Staubach was asked about the last ditch throw that he said, "I closed my eyes and said a Hail Mary." The next day, all reports on the game led with the miracle of Staubach's "Hail Mary" pass that delivered the Cowboys from the loss.

In the aftermath of one of the most gut-wrenching games to watch for Vikings fans, Fran Tarkenton learned that the stress had been too much for his father to watch and he had died of a heart attack in front of his television at his home in Atlanta. The sole consolation for Vikings fans was that the Cowboys would lose in the Super Bowl to the Pittsburgh Steelers.

The First Vikings Coach

Six years before becoming the second coach in Minnesota Vikings history, Bud Grant came close to becoming the first.

Late in the summer of 1960, the Minnesota expansion NFL franchise named Bert Rose as its first general manager. His first major task was to select the team's first coach. By mid-December, four candidates had emerged—Northwestern University coach Ara Parseghian, Vikings' scout John Thomas, Philadelphia Eagles quarterback Norm Van Brocklin and former Minnesota Gopher and Minneapolis Laker Bud Grant, who had just completed his fourth season as the Winnipeg (Canadian Football League) coach.

In the December 19 issue of the *Minneapolis Morning Tribune*, Rose denied that Van Brocklin, who was preparing for the Eagles' appearance in the NFL Championship game (against Green Bay), had been offered the job. His denial came one day after Van Brocklin had thrown two touchdown passes to lead the Eagles to a 36–28 victory over the Washington Redskins in their regular-season finale.

A week later—on December 26—Van Brocklin passed for 204 yards and a touchdown in the Eagles' 17–13 victory over the Packers in the NFL Championship game. After the game, Van Brocklin, three months shy of his 35th birthday, told reporters he was "through as a player."

The day after the game, Eagles coach Buck Shaw announced his resignation and Van Brocklin was immediately mentioned as a candidate to replace Shaw.

Over the next week, most of the attention of the Twin Cities media was focused on the University of Minnesota football team's first appearance in the Rose Bowl. On January 4, two days after the Gophers lost to Washington, a newspaper report said that the Eagles had offered Van Brocklin a contract (as a player) for the 1961 season.

Two weeks later, in the January 18 issue of the *Minneapolis Morning Tribune*, Sid Hartman wrote, "Indications are Bud Grant may withdraw as candidate of the Minnesota Vikings coaching job."

Hartman wrote that Grant had met with Vikings officials the previous Friday (January 13) and that Van Brocklin had interviewed on January 17 (Parseghian had interviewed in December and Thomas had recently been interviewed).

On January 18, the Vikings named Van Brocklin, who had just completed his 12th season in the NFL (he was named All-Pro for the fourth time in 1960), coach and signed him to a three-year contract.

Van Brocklin went on to coach the Vikings for their first six seasons. He resigned following the 1966 season, which saw the Vikings lose five of their last six games to finish with a 4–9–1 record. The team was 29–51–4 under Van Brocklin.

In early February 1967, within a 24-hour span, quarterback Fran Tarkenton requested a trade and Van Brocklin resigned.

On March 10, 1967, three days after Tarkenton had been traded to the New York Giants, Grant was named the Vikings coach.

The First Starting Quarterback

In their final exhibition game before their first NFL regular-season game, the Minnesota Vikings lost to the Los Angeles Rams 21–17 at Metropolitan Stadium.

The Rams led 21–3 before the Vikings mounted a fourth-quarter comeback behind rookie quarterback Fran Tarkenton. Tarkenton ran for one touchdown and passed for another as the *Minneapolis Morning Tribune* described his efforts "a bold bid for the No. 1 job."

But a week later, in the Vikings' NFL debut, Vikings coach Norm Van Brocklin elected to go with veteran George Shaw as his starting quarterback against the Chicago Bears. Shaw, who was in his seventh year in the NFL, completed two of three passes for 22 yards and directed the Vikings to a field goal, but with the Vikings leading 3–0 late in the first quarter, he was replaced by Tarkenton. Just two minutes into the second quarter, Tarkenton threw his first touchdown pass (to Bob Schnelker).

After leading the Vikings to the surprising 37–13 victory over the Bears, Tarkenton was named the Vikings' starter for their second game. Things didn't go as well for Tarkenton and the Vikings in week two, as

Tarkenton completed just 8 of 24 passes for 117 yards in a 21–7 loss to the Dallas Cowboys.

Shaw returned to the starting lineup in week three and made two more starts before Tarkenton moved into the starting job for good. Shaw didn't return to the Vikings in 1962, spending his final season in pro football with Denver of the AFL.

Ole Haugsrud

The Duluth Eskimos—owned by Ole Haugsrud, who had taken over the team in 1923 when it was called the Duluth Kelleys—were struggling financially, like the rest of the league, when Haugsrud got an idea. His plan included convincing a former high school friend of his—who was currently playing major league baseball—to come play for the Eskimos.

His friend, Willow River native Ernie Nevers, had played college football at Stanford. While at Stanford, Nevers had earned 11 varsity letters in four sports to earn consideration as one of the top all-around college athletes in U.S. history.

In the summer of 1926, Haugsrud offered Nevers, who was pitching for the St. Louis Browns of the American League (AL), $15,000 and a percentage of the gate receipts to play for the Eskimos. After Nevers agreed to join the Eskimos, Haugsrud called the team "Ernie Nevers' Eskimos."

Nevers was joining a team whose 15-man roster included future Pro Football Hall of Fame members Walt Kiesling and Johnny "Blood" McNally.

The Eskimos opened the 1926 season with a 7–0 victory at home over the Kansas City Cowboys. Haugsrud figured that because of the team's star players, he could make more money playing a series of exhibitions and games on the road, so the season opener was the Eskimos' only home game of the season.

After their season-opening victory, the Eskimos embarked on a 25-game, 117-day barnstorming tour and didn't return home until February 5, 1927. During the tour, the team played 13 league games and 12 exhibitions. In one eight-day stretch, they played five games. Nevers, the team's star attraction, rarely left the field. He missed just 29 minutes of play the entire season, and the Eskimos went 14–8–3 on the tour.

The next season, the Eskimos played all of their games on the road, going 1–8. They folded following the 1928 season.

Haugsrud sold the rights to his dormant franchise in 1929, and the NFL promised him that if a future NFL franchise was granted to Minnesota, he would have the first option to buy. In 1960, he became part of the Minnesota ownership group that was granted an NFL expansion franchise.

Haugsrud and Nevers, who was elected to the Pro Football Hall of Fame, both passed away in 1976.

The Hunt for a Pro Football Team

The period between 1952 and 1958 was one of disappointment for the Minnesotans who had hoped to lure either a major league baseball team or a pro football team to the state. Several major league baseball teams flirted with the idea of relocating to Minnesota, but nothing came of it. While being rebuffed by major league baseball, Minnesota was also being ignored by the NFL.

That changed in 1959. A group of businessmen, frustrated by the NFL's reluctance to consider expansion (the league's size hadn't changed since it had absorbed three teams from the All-American Football Conference in 1950), announced on August 14 that they were forming a second professional league, which would begin play in 1960 with eight teams.

One of the charter franchises in the new league—which was going to be called the American Football League—was awarded to Minnesota. The other seven franchises were awarded to Boston, Buffalo, Dallas, Denver, Houston, Los Angeles and New York.

There was a second development in 1959. The Chicago Cardinals, who were primarily ignored in their hometown because of the more successful Chicago Bears, played two of their "home" games at Metropolitan Stadium in Bloomington, one of the places they were considering moving to.

While the upstart league was conducting its first meeting, rumors began circulating that the Minnesota franchise was going to withdraw because it was going to be awarded an NFL expansion team. During a following meeting, Max Winter withdrew from the Minnesota group.

The next day, the league held its first player draft and the remaining members of the Minnesota group—Bill Boyer and H.P. Skoglund—selected players for the Minnesota franchise.

At the AFL's next meeting, in early December in Dallas, league owners agreed to allow the Minnesota franchise to withdraw from the league. The AFL replaced it by awarding a franchise to Oakland.

In January 1960, the NFL awarded expansion franchises to Dallas, which would begin play in 1960, and Minnesota, which would join the league in 1961.

A Little Revenge

In January 1970, the NFL Champion Minnesota Vikings and the AFL Champion Kansas City Chiefs met in New Orleans for Super Bowl IV. In the last Super Bowl pitting the AFL against the NFL champions—the AFL merged into the NFL following the 1969 season—the Chiefs defeated the Vikings 23–7.

The loss—the first of four Super Bowl losses in an eight-year span for the Vikings—was made memorable by Kansas City coach Hank Stram. Stram wore a microphone during the game and his laughter and ridicule of the Vikings was captured by NFL Films.

The Vikings got a little revenge eight months later when they opened the 1970 regular season with a 27–10 victory over the Chiefs before 47,900 fans at Metropolitan Stadium. In their pre-game meeting on that Sunday morning, the Vikings watched, for the first time as a group, the replay of Super Bowl IV.

Biggest Story in Minnesota Sports History, Circa 1989

The Vikings started the 1989 season with a 3–2 record, and rumors had started circulating that the winless Dallas Cowboys were considering trading star running back Herschel Walker. Vikings general manager Mike Lynn thought Walker, who had rushed for more than 1500 yards the previous season, was the player who could take the Vikings to the next level.

On October 12, after several days of negotiations, Lynn and the Cowboys reached an agreement on a trade that would send the 27-year old Walker to the Vikings. In the deal, the Vikings sent the Cowboys five players and eight conditional draft choices in exchange for Walker and four draft choices.

Three days after the trade, which the *Minneapolis Star Tribune* described as "the most-covered—if not the biggest story—in Minnesota sports history," Walker made a spectacular debut for the Vikings. He rushed for 148 yards—the first Viking to rush for more than 100 yards in 30 games dating to the 1987 season—to lead the Vikings to a 26–14 victory over the Green Bay Packers. The trade sparked the Vikings to the NFC Central title (with a 10–6 record), but the season came to abrupt end with a 41–13 loss to the San Francisco 49ers in the first round of the playoffs.

The team opened the 1990 season with just one victory in the first seven games and struggled to a 6–10 record while missing the playoffs. Following the season, Lynn left the organization and Roger Headrick took over the day-to-day operation of the team.

The Vikings went 8–8 in 1991 but missed the playoffs again. Walker became a casualty of those two lost seasons. Despite leading the Vikings in rushing in each of his three seasons with the team, he was released by the team in May 1992.

The release of Walker after less than three seasons fueled talk of what a disaster the trade had been. After acquiring Walker, the Vikings did not have a first-round draft choice for the next four years. Meanwhile, the Cowboys, who had gone 3–13 the year before the trade and 1–15 in 1989, had used the trade to rebuild quickly. They improved to 7–9 in 1990, 11–5 in 1991, 13–3 in 1992 and went 12–4 in both the 1993 and 1994 seasons. The Cowboys advanced to the Super Bowl following the 1992, 1993 and 1995 seasons—winning all three.

After being released by the Vikings, Walker joined the Philadelphia Eagles and rushed for 1070 yards in 1992 and played two more seasons in the NFL. After retiring from the NFL, he continued his athletic endeavors. In 2002, he was a member of the U.S. Olympic bobsled team, finishing seventh in the two-man bobsled at the Olympics that year. In 2010, at the age of 48, Walker began a career as a mixed martial arts fighter.

Changing of the Guard

In early 1992, the Minnesota Vikings did something the franchise hadn't done in a quarter of a century: they hired a coach from outside the organization. Stanford coach Dennis Green, 42, was the first coach hired externally since 1967, replacing head coach Jerry Burns, who had stepped down after six seasons.

Green had spent three seasons at Stanford. Prior to that position, he had been an assistant to San Francisco 49ers coach Bill Walsh for three years and the head coach at Northwestern for five years.

At his introductory press conference, Green, just the second African American to become a head coach in the modern NFL era (Art Shell became the coach of the Los Angeles Raiders in 1989), said, "There's a new sheriff in town."

An Abrupt End to a Memorable Decade

Green led the Vikings to the playoffs in five of his first six seasons. In his seventh season, in 1998, the Vikings went 15–1 and reached the NFC championship game, where they were routed by the New York Giants 41–0.

In 2001, Green's 10th season, the Vikings had stumbled to a 5–10 record with one game remaining in the season when Green, who had two years remaining on his contract, was relieved of his coaching duties.

Taking Ownership

In 1997, the NFL was putting pressure on the Vikings' 10-person ownership group to reorganize so that one person owned at least 30 percent of the team's stock. In October 1997, the team's board of directors announced the team was for sale.

Five months later, author Tom Clancy offered to buy the team for $200 million. But Clancy's bid—he would need to put up $60 million (30 percent of the purchase price) to become the lead investor—quickly fell apart.

Clancy was going through a divorce, and court documents listed his net worth as $13.6 million. He had intended to invest only $5 million in the deal, and in May 1998, he withdrew his offer.

Three months later, a buyer was found. Texas billionaire Red McCombs agreed to purchase the team for $246 million (which included about $40 million in assumed debt). Less than seven years later, McCombs sold the team to a group headed by New Jersey real estate developer Zygi Wilf for $600 million.

Korey Stringer

In 1995, the Vikings selected Korey Stringer, an offensive lineman from Ohio State, in the first round of the NFL draft. The 6-foot-5, 335-pound Stringer moved into the Vikings' starting lineup in the second game of his rookie season and remained there for the next six seasons. Following the 2000 season, he was named to the Pro Bowl.

In July 2001, Stringer reported to Mankato for his seventh Vikings training camp. On the second day of training camp, he became ill after the team's morning workout. He was hospitalized, and early the next morning, he died from complications of heat stroke. He was 27. His death was the first in an NFL training camp since 1979.

Embarrassing Times

In late February 2005, the Minnesota Vikings announced they were trading receiver Randy Moss to the Oakland Raiders for a first-round draft pick and linebacker Napoleon Harris. Owner Red McCombs said the trade was necessary because Moss and coach Mike Tice weren't getting along; after considering firing Tice, McCombs decided instead to trade Moss.

Two weeks after the trade, the NFL announced that Tice was being investigated for scalping Super Bowl tickets. Tice originally denied the charge, which had been brought to the NFL's attention by a former Vikings player. But Tice eventually admitted to the scalping, and he was fined $100,000 by the league.

In May, there was more embarrassment for the franchise when it was reported that Vikings running back Onterrio Smith had been detained at Minneapolis–St. Paul International Airport the previous month. He had been stopped after trying to sneak a device used to beat drug tests through airport security. Smith, who had been suspended for four games in 2004 for a violation of the league's drug policy, reportedly was facing a drug test when he was caught with the "Original Whizzinator." The NFL treated the situation as a positive drug test for Smith and suspended him for the entire 2005 season.

Smith, who had rushed for 579 yards in 2003 and 544 yards in 2004 (despite missing four games), would not play in the NFL again—the Vikings released him in April 2006, one month before his suspension was over. He signed with Winnipeg of the CFL that May but was cut by the team before the season started.

The Love Boat

The Vikings had reached the second round of the playoffs in 2004 and looked good in the 2005 preseason—winning three of four games. So, when they opened the 2005 season with just one victory in their first four games, fans were critical of quarterback Daunte Culpepper and the rest of the team's on-field performance.

In week 5 of the season—a bye week for the Vikings—the team would give fans even more to criticize. On October 11, Twin Cities media outlets reported that, two days earlier, members of the Vikings had rented two yachts for an outing on Lake Minnetonka. The outing was described as a sex party—with some women being flown in from out of state—and was named the "Love Boat" scandal.

Culpepper was one of the players implicated in the scandal. Ultimately, he was never charged and only several fines were handed out in the aftermath of the outing. Still, it caused a lot of embarrassment for owner Zygi Wilf, who was in his first year as the team's owner.

In their first game after the "Love Boat," the Vikings lost at Chicago to fall to 1–4. But they regrouped, winning six consecutive games in one stretch, and took an 8–7 record into their season-finale against the Chicago Bears at the Metrodome.

On January 1, 2006, the Vikings defeated the Bears, who had already clinched the NFC North title, to finish the season with a 9–7 record (equaling their best record in five seasons under Tice). Less than an hour after the game, Tice was fired as coach. Wilf conceded that Tice was fired more for the off-field issues than he was for his 32–33 record and reaching the playoffs just once in five seasons.

Consistency

In their first 50 seasons in the NFL, the Minnesota Vikings have played two teams—the Chicago Bears and the Green Bay Packers—more times than they have played any other team. During the 2010 season, the Vikings played the Bears and the Packers for the 100th time each.

Rivalries

From their first meeting in 1961, the Packers were the Vikings' biggest rival. The Packers won the first game between the two teams and dominated the early years of the rivalry by winning 11 of the first 14 meetings between the teams, but going into the 2010 season, they held a slim 49–48–1 edge. Of the 98 games played between the two teams, 43 have been decided by seven points or less.

In 50 seasons, the Vikings have endured only seven losses worse than the 28-point margin present in their game against the Packers on November 21, which ended in a score of 31–3. The game also marked the 295th consecutive NFL start by Vikings quarterback Brett Favre, who was starting a game in the series for the 36th time.

The loss, which dropped the Vikings to 3–7, became even more significant the next day when Vikings coach Brad Childress was fired. The firing came less than a year after Childress, who was in his fifth season as the Vikings coach, had coached the Vikings to a 12–4 record and a spot in the NFC Championship game. By coincidence, the loss dropped Childress' record against the Packers to 3–7, and he was replaced by defensive coordinator Leslie Frazier, who became the eighth coach in team history. Childress had a 39–35 regular-season record (1–2 in the playoffs) in his four and a half seasons as the Vikings coach.

More Rivalry Facts

The loss to the Packers in the 100th meeting in the series left the Vikings with a 25–24 record against the Packers in games played in Minnesota. Each team won 10 times in the 20 games played at Metropolitan

Stadium, and each team has won 14 times in the 28 games played at the Metrodome.

During the 21 seasons they shared Metropolitan Stadium with the Minnesota Twins, the Vikings had to move only one home game because of a scheduling conflict with the Twins. On October 5, 1969, with the Minnesota Twins playing host to the Baltimore Orioles in the AL Championship Series, the Vikings were forced to move their home game against the Green Bay Packers to the University of Minnesota's Memorial Stadium. Before a crowd of 60,740—the largest home crowd for the Vikings in their first 21 seasons—the Vikings won 19–7.

The Vikings played only one other game at the University of Minnesota's Memorial Stadium: on August 8, 1971, the team hosted the New England Patriots in a preseason game. The Patriots won the game 17–10 before 31,813 fans.

The largest regular-season crowd for the Vikings at Metropolitan Stadium was 49,784—a sellout for football at the stadium—which happened on several occasions, but most recently on December 10, 1972, when the Vikings lost 23–7 to the Packers.

The Packers have a 27–23–1 advantage over the Vikings in games played in Wisconsin. The Packers have an 18–17–1 edge in games played at Green Bay's Lambeau Field and are 9–6 against the Vikings in games played at Milwaukee's County Stadium.

Of the first 100 meetings between the Packers and the Vikings, only one game was in the playoffs. Following the 2004 season, the Vikings defeated the Packers 31–17 in an NFC Wild Card game in Green Bay.

The Vikings and the Chicago Bears have also met just once in the playoffs. Following the 1994 season, the Bears defeated the Vikings 35–18 in a first-round playoff game at the Metrodome. Going into the 2010 season, the Vikings held a 52–44–2 lead in the series.

The Vikings have played the Bears, the Packers and the Detroit Lions at least twice in every regular season (except one) since joining the NFL in 1961. They played each team just once during the 1982 season, which was shortened to nine games because of a labor dispute.

Because the Vikings and Lions have never played each other in the playoffs, they played only 97 times going into the 2010 season, with the Vikings leading the series 65–30–2.

Weathered Out

The Minnesota Vikings' 2010 season—their 50th season in Minnesota—will be remembered for several things: the firing of coach Brad Childress, their 6–10 record (and first last-place finish since 1990) and the weather.

The Vikings had three games impacted by the weather in December. Their home game against the New York Giants, scheduled for December 12, was postponed because a snowstorm damaged the roof of the Metrodome. The game was moved to Detroit and played the next day. The Metrodome's roof couldn't be repaired in time for the Vikings' next home game—December 20 against the Chicago Bears—so that game was played (in a snowstorm) at the University of Minnesota's TCF Bank Stadium.

Consequently, in a three-week span, the Vikings had three consecutive "home" games and each one was played in a different stadium: December 5 vs. Buffalo in Minneapolis, December 13 vs. New York in Detroit and December 20 vs. Chicago at TCF Bank Stadium.

The Vikings had one more game affected by the weather. Their December 26 game in Philadelphia was postponed two days because of a blizzard. On December 28, the Vikings defeated the Eagles 24–14 in the first NFL game played on a Tuesday in 64 years. The last time two NFL teams played on a Tuesday was October 1, 1946, when the New York Giants defeated the Boston Yankees 17–0.

Minnesota Football Quick Facts

- Since joining the NFL in 1961, the Vikings have been one of the most successful franchises with the fifth-highest winning percentage.
- The Vikings are also known as the Vikes, Purple Pride, the Purple People Eaters, and Purple and Gold.
- The Vikings played their first playoff game on December 22, 1968, in a 24–14 defeat by the Baltimore Colts in the Western Conference Championship game. Their first playoff win came one year later when they defeated the LA Rams 23–20 in the Western Conference Championship.

- The Vikings' first winning season came three years after joining the NFL, in 1964, when they finished with an 8–5–1 record.
- The official song of the Minnesota Vikings is called "Skol, Vikings!" and it is attributed to Red McCloud. "Skol" is the Scandinavian word for "cheer."
- Since the Vikings joined the NFL in 1961, 15 players who once wore the Viking horns have been enshrined in the Pro Football Hall of Fame. They are Hugh McElhenny (1970), Fran Tarkenton (1986), Jim Langer (1987), Alan Page (1988), Jan Stenerud (1991), Bud Grant (1994), Jim Finks (1995), Paul Krause (1998), Ron Yary (2001), Dave Casper (2002), Carl Eller (2004), Warren Moon (2006), Gary Zimmerman (2008), Randall McDaniel (2009) and John Randle (2010).
- The Minnesota Vikings have retired the numbers of only six players who have made a significant mark in the history of the club. These are Fran Tarkenton's number 10, Mick Tingelhoff's number 53, Jim Marshall's number 70, Korey Stringer's number 77, Cris Carter's number 80 and Alan Page's number 88.
- Former Minnesota Vikings wide receiver Ahmad Rashad (1976–1982) married *The Cosby Show* actress Phylicia Ayers-Allen in 1985. He proposed to her on national television during the NBC pre-game show for a Thanksgiving Day football game.
- Former Vikings defensive tackle Alan Page received his law degree from the University of Minnesota Law School in 1978 and upon graduation began

working for the Lindquist and Vennum law firm in Minneapolis outside the football season. When his football career officially ended, Page practiced law full time, and by 1992 he was elected as an Associate Justice of the Minnesota Supreme Court.

Minnesota Football Quotables

"You get to a point at 40 years old that you know exactly what you want to do—if you want to play football or not. And that's why I've been critical of this guy. Because it's so unfair to your teammates, it's unfair to your coaches, it's unfair to the city, the organization, that you keep leaving people hung out to dry like that. I've never understood Brett Favre. I just think he loves the media attention. At 40 years old, you know if you want to grind through an 18-week season. If I was a teammate of his, I'd probably be a little ticked off he's not in training camp."

–New England Patriots safety Rodney Harrison on the ever-changing status of Brett Favre

"If football taught me anything about business, it is that you win the game one play at a time."

–Fran Tarkenton, former Vikings quarterback

"Success, in my view, is the willingness to strive for something you really want. The person not reaching the top is no less a success than the one who achieved it, if they both sweated blood, sweat and tears and overcame obstacles and fears. The failure to be perfect does not mean you're not a success."

–Fran Tarkenton

"I went a different route, but I ended up playing a lot longer than I thought I would or that I could."
—Warren Moon, former Vikings quarterback on his long career in pro football

"Never in my wildest dreams, when we sat here last year, would I have thought I would've played the way I did. I mean, look at 18 years previous. I never played that good."
—Brett Favre after rejoining the Vikings for the 2010 season

Chapter Two

The Twins at Bat

Baseball at the Metrodome

Opened on April 3, 1982, the 55,883-seat stadium in downtown Minneapolis stands out with its distinctive white fiberglass fabric roof acting as a brilliant beacon for the city's sports fans. Being a spectator in that bright, airy stadium is an experience like none other, and many players have said that the noise generated by 55,000 screaming fans under that amplifying dome is an experience that will leave your ears ringing for days.

This apparent amplification is a feature of the Metrodome that the hometown fans are very well aware of and use to the best of their abilities during games. During ball games, fans cheer at the most opportune moments to distract opposing teams to the point where players can't communicate with each other and batters lose their concentration. This home field advantage was one of the factors in the Minnesota Twins' magical run to the World Series in 1987. Backed by their crazed fans and the talents of Kirby

Puckett, the Twins rode the crowd's support through the season and all the way to the championship.

"Minnesota had the fifth-best record in the American League that year. And they proceeded to kick our ass around that lunatic homer dome, where you can't see a fly ball or hear it come off the bat," said St. Louis Cardinals manager Whitey Herzog. The Twins ended up winning all their home games, played in the noisy Metrodome, and losing all the games played in St. Louis.

Just so you have an idea of how loud the Metrodome can be, decibel levels were measured at a maximum of 125 during the 1987 World Series, comparable to the noise output of a jet engine.

A New Home

The Metrodome hosted another World Series in 1991, and fans got to celebrate another championship under the noisy dome. It was the perfect stadium for the times, built to get fans into their seats, watch the game and get back out again. But after 27 years, the stadium had begun to show its age, and in the era of modern stadiums with every amenity under the sun, the Twins organization decided they needed a new home venue of their own to catch up with the rest of the majors.

The Twins abandoned the Metrodome in 2009 for the beautiful Target Field for the start of the 2010 season. It was a bittersweet goodbye to the old, noisy Metrodome, but the $545-million, 41,000-seat stadium meets the needs of every fan, whether corporate or a family. The Twins no longer have the dome overhead to act as an extra player, but the new stadium brings a different feeling to the ball club and will hopefully establish a winning tradition of its own. The Twins got off to a good start in their new home, winning the AL Central Division title in 2010.

The Magnificent Kirby Puckett

From the moment he put on a Twins jersey in 1984, Kirby Puckett was an instant fan favorite and remained in the hearts of Minnesota sports fans until he was forced to retire. A young Puckett seemed destined for greatness when he stepped up to the plate for his first big league game, against the California Angels, and ended up going 4 for 5.

Shorter than most baseball players, at 5 feet 8 inches tall, Puckett stood out from the bigger athletes, but what he lacked in stature he made up with pure muscle power. With an incredibly muscular upper torso, Puckett appeared like a mini-Hulk out on the field, and he quickly began to earn the loyalty of fans with his powerful batting and lightning fast center field heroics. As a rookie in 1984, he hit a respectable .296 with 165 hits in 128 games.

Just two seasons later, in 1986, Puckett emerged as the Twins' superstar and one of the league's premier players. His offensive skills were unquestioned with his batting average of .328, and his defensive talents could not be ignored. Countless times, batters would send the ball deep into center field, but Kirby would always be there waiting for it. If someone managed to knock a ball toward the gap, the evening's highlight reels would often show Puckett sprinting at the pace of an Olympic athlete and leaping into the air to make the catch. This occurred on such a regular basis during the 1986 season that the league awarded Puckett his first Golden Glove award for his defensive prowess.

There is no doubt that without the heroics of Kirby Puckett on the field during the 1987 season, the Twins would not have made it into the postseason. While the Twins had a solid lineup of players, no other regular player hit over .300 that season. Kirby finished the 1987 season with a batting average of .332 and a team-leading 207 hits, and the Twins won their first World Series championship.

The Twins just managed to beat out the Kansas City Chiefs for the AL West Division leadership and made it into the playoffs that year. Kirby was relatively silent through the first test for the Twins, but the team managed to pull together and defeat the Detroit Tigers four games to one in the series to win the AL. In the World Series, Puckett would have to play like he did during the regular season if the Twins were to have any chance against the St. Louis Cardinals.

It was a long seven-game series but Puckett and the Twins held firm in their belief that they would win it all. Puckett finished the series with a batting average of .357 and was responsible for driving in the game-tying run in the seventh and final game of the series.

The late 1980s brought more good news for Puckett when he recorded his best career stats in 1988, hitting .356 with 24 home runs and 121 runs batted in (RBI). The fortunes of the Twins would wax and wane in 1989 and 1990, but Puckett was always the model of consistency at the plate and in the field.

The team made it back to prominence in 1991 and finished the season strong with a berth in the playoffs against the heavily favored Toronto Blue Jays. Puckett hit an incredible .429 and six RBI, leading the Twins past the Jays. But the highlight of the postseason for Puckett came in game six of the World Series against the Atlanta Braves. The Twins were in a must-win situation, down 3–2 in the series. The game went into extra innings and in the bottom of the eleventh inning, Puckett hit a game-winning home run to keep the Twins' hopes alive. The image of Puckett rounding the bases with his arms outstretched is one of legend in both baseball and Twins history. The Twins carried the momentum into game seven and finished the Braves off with a close 1–0 win for the franchise's second championship.

Goodbye, Kirby

After the 1991 World Series, the fates of the Minnesota Twins and Kirby Puckett mutually began to take a turn for the worse. The Twins failed to make the postseason for the next several seasons, and Puckett's performance at the plate suffered. The 1995 season started off well for Puckett, with him seemingly finding his rhythm at the plate once again, but he was stopped short by a wild toss that broke his jaw and ended his season. Then, in the spring of 1996, Puckett woke up one morning and found he could not see out of his right eye. He was diagnosed with glaucoma and would never again play professional baseball. The news hit Puckett and the Twins organization hard, and it was difficult for Puckett to maintain his composure during his press conference on July 12, 1996.

"Baseball's been a great part of my life," he said during the conference. "But now it's time for me to close this chapter of this book in baseball and go on with part two of my life. Kirby Puckett's going to be all right. Don't worry about me...."

Kirby Puckett left the field, but in 1997 his name was added to the list of Minnesota Twins greats when his jersey was retired by the team. Puckett would eventually move to Arizona with his fiancée and family in 2003.

Just three years later, on March 5, 2006, Puckett suffered a massive stroke and died the following day after being disconnected from life support. A week later, family and friends invited the public to the Metrodome for a memorial service for the fallen Minnesota legend. Some 20,000 fans showed up to pay their respects to their baseball hero, who was taken too soon.

Minnesota Man Kent Hrbek

All athletes have their own way of relaxing before a crucial game. Some listen to music, some like to be left alone with their thoughts; Kent Hrbek of the Minnesota Twins went duck hunting.

The day of the deciding game seven of the World Series, Hrbek woke up before dawn, put on his hunting gear, flung his gun over his shoulder and drove out into the wilderness to shoot some ducks. In a strange twist, he and his friends shot four ducks that morning; later that day, Hrbek and the Twins scored four runs in a 4–2 World Series victory over the Cardinals.

Throughout his career with the Minnesota Twins, he remained a consistent big-game hitter. He won the World Series with the Twins in 1987 and 1991 and retired from professional baseball in 1994 because of nagging injury problems. One year after leaving the Twins, his number 14 was retired, and in 1996 he was inducted into the Minnesota Sports Hall of Fame.

Now Hrbek spends the majority of his spare time out in the woods and on lakes, pursuing his true passion, and hosts his own outdoor sports television program called *Kent Hrbek's Outdoors*.

In Their Own Backyard

In June 2001, the Minnesota Twins had the number one pick in Major League Baseball's (MLB) annual draft. Coming off eight consecutive losing seasons, they were under pressure to make a pick that would help the team. Adding even more pressure to the financially strapped, small-market Twins (which would be threatened with contraction by the MLB later that year) was whether they would be able to sign their first choice. Twice in the previous nine years, the Twins had failed to sign their first-round pick—Jason Varitek in 1993 and Travis Lee in 1996. In addition to those two picks, the Twins' top picks in 1998, 1999 and 2000 failed to help the team.

Most observers thought an argument could be made for any one of four potential draft choices—University of Southern California pitcher Mark Prior, considered the top college pitching prospect in 10 years, Georgia Tech third baseman Mark Teixeira, Middle Tennessee State pitcher Dewon Brazelton and Minnesota high school legend Joe Mauer.

Signing any of the four was expected to be tough. The Twins apparently narrowed their choice to either Prior or Mauer.

Prior, who was considered to be the most advanced of the potential picks (the Twins were in dire need of pitching help), was thought to be asking for a signing bonus in the $10- to $15-million range. Mauer, despite between a hometown favorite, wasn't going to be easy, either: as a three-sport star at Cretin-Derham Hall High School in St. Paul, he had options. Among them, he had a scholarship offer to play football for Florida State.

In the end, the Twins selected Mauer, and negotiations lasted about a month before he signed for a $5.15-million signing bonus. On April 5, 2004, after three seasons in the minors and still two weeks shy of his 21st birthday, Mauer made his major league debut. In 2006, he became the first catcher in AL history to win the batting title, and two years later, he won his second batting title.

Changing Times

In July 1959, a group of New York businessmen announced their intention to form a third baseball major league. After getting annoyed with MLB's reluctance to expand, the group, which included long-time MLB executive Branch Rickey and a lawyer named William Shea, decided to form the Continental League.

Their frustration was understandable. Between 1902 and 1952, the AL and National League (NL) consisted of the same 16 franchises in the same 11 cities. The Boston Braves' move to Milwaukee for the 1953 season was the first franchise re-location in 50 years and caused the first change in the stable American Association in nearly 50 years.

The move gave civic leaders in Minnesota the hope that they would be able to secure a major league team as well. During the 1950s, Midway Stadium in St. Paul and Metropolitan Stadium in Bloomington were built to help lure a major league team to the area. At least four teams considered moving to the Twin Cities: the New York Giants of the NL and the Philadelphia Athletics, St. Louis Browns and Washington Senators of the AL.

In July 1958, owner Calvin Griffith reportedly was ready to ask for permission to move the Washington

Senators to Minnesota. Two months later, he announced the team would stay in Washington. In October 1959, a national publication reported that he was ready to move his team to Minnesota for the 1960 season. Again, he changed his mind.

After Griffith's second flirtation with Minnesota, Minnesotans mostly gave up on the Senators and turned their attention to the Continental League. The league, which announced it would begin play in 1961, continued to woo Minnesota. In January 1960, Rickey visited Minnesota and told reporters that the area was important to the league, which intended to field teams in Atlanta, Buffalo, Dallas, Denver, Houston, New York and Toronto.

Finally, in July 1960, the NL announced that it would expand to 10 teams. Shortly after that, the AL also announced it would expand by two teams.

On August 2, 1960, the Continental League announced it was folding. The League said it had received a promise that the AL and the NL would expand into cities that would have been part of the Continental League.

On October 26, the AL announced that the Washington Senators would relocate to Minnesota for the 1961 season.

Compromise

When the Washington Senators relocated to Minnesota, there was much debate over what the team would be called.

Because the team would be playing in suburban Bloomington, a choice of "Twin Cities" or using either Minneapolis or St. Paul didn't make sense. Owner Calvin Griffith, sensitive to the rivalry between Minneapolis and St. Paul, settled on "Minnesota Twins" for the team's name. It makes sense, but at the time it was unprecedented. The Twins were the first major league team to use the name of a state instead of the name of a city in front of the team's nickname.

The Franchise's First Star

Harmon Killebrew made his major league debut with the Washington Senators in 1954, at the age of 18. Spending most of his first five seasons in professional baseball in the minor leagues, he appeared in just 113 games (hitting 11 home runs) with the Senators between 1954 and 1958.

Killebrew's breakthrough season came in 1959. In his first season as a regular in the Senators' lineup, he led the AL with 42 home runs. In 1960, the Senators' final season in Washington, D.C., he hit 31 home runs.

After the Senators relocated to Minnesota for the 1961 season, Killebrew continued to hit home runs. In the team's first 10 seasons in Minnesota, he averaged 40 home runs per season while winning the AL home run title five times.

Killebrew hit 28 home runs in 1971—surpassing 500 career home runs at mid-season—and hit 26 home runs in 1972. It was the final time he would hit at least 20 home runs in his career.

In 1973, injuries limited the 37-year-old player to just 69 games and he hit only five home runs. In 1974, he appeared in 122 games, but he hit only 13 home runs with a .222 batting average.

Following the season, Twins owner Calvin Griffith didn't think Killebrew was an every-day player any more. He offered Killebrew three options: become a Twins' coach, serve as manager and designated hitter for the Twins' top farm team (Tacoma) or be released. In January 1975, Griffith amended his offer to Killebrew, saying he could be a player-coach (serving as a pinch-hitter) for the Twins for $50,000.

Killebrew still wanted to be a full-time player and in mid-January asked for his release. After hitting 559 home runs in his 21 seasons with the organization (84 with the Senators and 475 with the Twins), he signed a one-year contract with the Kansas City Royals.

The 1975 season would be Killebrew's final season of professional baseball. In 106 games with the Royals, he hit 14 home runs—two against the Twins— and drove in 44 runs while batting just .199.

On May 4 in Bloomington, Killebrew hit his first home run against his former team—a two-run shot in the first inning off Twins lefthander Vic Albury—in a game won by the Twins 6–3. Ironically, his other home run against the Twins was the final home run of his career. On September 18—a day game with just 3201 fans in attendance—Killebrew hit a solo home run off Twins' rookie Eddie Bane in the second inning, the 573rd home run of his career.

Tony O.

As a rookie with the Minnesota Twins in 1964, Tony Oliva hit .323 to win the AL batting title. In 1965, he won the AL batting title again to become the first player to win batting titles in his first two years in the big league.

In 1973, the AL adopted the designated hitter rule, allowing a player to take the pitcher's place in the batting lineup. On opening day, the first player to bat as a designated hitter in an AL game was Ron Blomberg of the New York Yankees. Later that day, Oliva became the first player to hit a home run as a designated hitter when he hit a two-run home run off Catfish Hunter in the Twins' 8–3 victory in Oakland.

Billy Martin

The Minnesota Twins have employed 12 managers during their first 50 seasons in Minnesota, and all but three of them managed the team for at least one full season.

Billy Martin is known for having the third shortest stint as the manager of the Twins, being fired after one season (1969) despite leading the team to 97 victories and the AL West Division title.

But the season ended with the Twins being swept in the AL Championships Series by the Baltimore Orioles, and Twins owner Calvin Griffith reportedly was upset that Martin had used Bob Miller as his starting pitcher in game three (instead of Jim Kaat). Miller had lasted less than two innings in the Orioles' 11–2 victory.

That wasn't the only factor working against Martin. During the regular season, he and one of his players (pitcher Dave Boswell) had been involved in a fight in a Detroit bar.

Martin was replaced by Bill Rigney, who led the Twins to the AL West Division title in 1970. Rigney lasted only two and a half seasons before being fired at midseason in 1972.

Martin went on to manage 15 more seasons in the big leagues with four teams—Detroit, Texas, Oakland and New York.

Arbitration

In five major league seasons, pitcher Dick Woodson compiled a forgettable 34–32 win-loss record. Unfortunately, it would be a contract dispute with Twins owner Calvin Griffith that made his big league career distinctive.

Woodson, who was paid $19,000 in 1973, asked for $28,500 for 1974. Griffith offered the 6-foot-5 right-hander $6,000 less. The dispute ended up being decided by a third party as Woodson, who was 28, became the first player in MLB history to go through an arbitration process.

The arbitrator ruled in favor of Woodson, prompting Griffith to tell a Minneapolis newspaper, "It made my stomach turn when I heard what Woodson got from the arbitrator."

One month into the 1974 season, Griffith traded Woodson to the New York Yankees. At the time of the trade, Woodson was 1–1 with a 4.33 earned run average (ERA) in five appearances. He went 1–2 in eight games for the Yankees to finish the season with a 2–3 record, and did not appear in the major league after the 1974 season.

Older than the State Itself

In August 1857, nine months before Minnesota achieved statehood, the first recorded baseball game in the state's history was played in Nininger (in Dakota County, southeast of St. Paul). This game is the village's only contribution to Minnesota history—after a financial panic later in the year, the town went into decline and eventually became a ghost town.

Ten years later, the first state tournament was held.

Professional baseball first appeared in Minnesota in 1877, when teams from Minneapolis and St. Paul appeared in the League Alliance, a loose collaboration of 13 teams.

The next professional baseball in the state was in 1884, when Minneapolis, St. Paul, Stillwater and Winona fielded teams in the Northwestern League. The Stillwater team included a 37-year-old New York native named Bud Fowler, who is generally recognized as the first African American to play professional baseball in America. Fowler, who began his baseball career in Massachusetts in 1878, batted .302 in 48 games. His career in organized baseball ended in 1895, when he batted .331 for a team in the Michigan State League at the age of 48.

A Decade of Change

In 1888, Minneapolis and St. Paul joined the Western Association, a league that would have a role in the evolution of the AL. In 1892, the Western Association changed its name to the Western League, and neither Minneapolis nor St. Paul fielded a team in 1893 because of financial difficulties. St. Paul was without a team in 1894 as well. But in 1895, professional baseball returned to St. Paul when Charles Comiskey moved his Sioux City franchise to St. Paul.

Five years later, there was another name change for the league when league president Ban Johnson changed its moniker to the American League. Comiskey also moved his franchise again in 1900—this time to Chicago, where the team would become known as the Chicago White Sox.

Minneapolis fielded a team in the AL's first season but had the lowest attendance in the league and was not going to be part of the AL in 1901. Minneapolis and St. Paul returned to a newer-formed Western League in 1901.

Change, then Stability

In 1902, Minneapolis and St. Paul joined a newly formed league called the American Association. The eight-team league would also field teams in Columbus (OH), Indianapolis (IN), Kansas City (MO), Louisville (KY), Milwaukee (WI) and Toledo (OH).

After 25 years of instability and constant change for professional baseball in the Twin Cities, the American Association brought an era of stability. For the next 50 years, the league's membership would remain unchanged (except for two years—1914 and 1915—when the Toledo team operated in Cleveland).

Natural Rivals

The Minneapolis Millers and the St. Paul Saints remained in the American Association for 59 seasons—until MLB arrived in Minnesota in the fall of 1960.

Because of their proximity, the teams were natural rivals. One minor league baseball historian wrote, "No sports rivalry was more bitterly contested over a longer period of time than the baseball competition between Minneapolis and St. Paul."

The teams met as many as 24 times per season, highlighted by holiday doubleheaders—on Memorial Day, the 4th of July and Labor Day—where a morning game was played in one park and an afternoon game in the other park. The holiday festivities occasionally got testy: on July 4, 1929, in Minneapolis, a bench-clearing brawl between the two teams needed 12 police officers to restore order.

During their 59 seasons in the American Association, the Millers and the Saints were the two winningest teams in the league. Each team finished first or second in the league's standings 16 times (each team won nine regular-season titles and each team also finished in second place seven times). In all, the teams played each other more than 1300 times as members of the American Association. The Saints won the all-time series 680–623, with 10 ties.

In October 1960, after several years of discussions, Washington Senators owner Calvin Griffith announced he was moving his team to Minnesota, ending the Minneapolis and St. Paul baseball rivalry.

A Familiar Face

In addition to the stability of the American Association, there was one other constant to professional baseball in the Twin Cities over the first 50 years of the 20th century: Mike Kelley.

Between 1902 and 1946, Kelley was associated with one of Minnesota's teams every year except for a brief period of a little over two years. He managed both the Minneapolis Millers and the St. Paul Saints. In 30 seasons as a minor league manager, he compiled a 2390–2102 record; his 2390 victories are third most in minor league baseball history. He also served as the owner of the Millers for many years before finally selling the franchise to the New York Giants of the NL in 1946.

Home Run King

In 1894, a 10-year veteran of professional baseball named Perry Werden joined the Minneapolis Millers of the Western League. The 6-foot-2, 220-pound player, whose nickname was "Moose," took an immediate liking to the Millers' compact home field, Athletic Park.

In his first season with the Millers, Werden, who had hit 51 home runs in his first 10 professional seasons (with a career high of 13 in 1887), slugged a professional baseball record 43 home runs and batted .417 in 114 games.

In 1895, Werden broke his own record by hitting 45 home runs and batting .428 in 125 games. His home run record would stand for 25 years, until Babe Ruth hit 54 home runs for the New York Yankees in 1920.

Werden hit 195 home runs in his 24-year career, which ended in 1908 (he was 43 years old).

Home Run King II

Between 1922 and 1928, Joe Hauser hit 76 home runs in six major league seasons. But in 1929, he was sent back to the minor leagues, never to play in the big league again.

In his first season with the Millers, in 1932, the left-handed hitting Hauser benefited from the short right-field fence at the Millers' home (Nicollet Park) and hit 49 home runs. His second season with the Millers would be better.

Despite not hitting a home run in his first nine games, Hauser had 32 home runs by the end of June. After hitting home runs in seven consecutive games in mid-July, he had 40. He hit his 50th in the Millers' 105th game, and on August 13, he broke the American

Association record of 54 (set by the Millers' Nick Cullop in 1930) with his 55th home run. A week later, he hit his 60th home run (in the Millers' 134th game) to become the first professional baseball player to hit at least 60 home runs in a season more than once.

After hitting his 60th, Hauser cooled off, hitting only two home runs in a two-week stretch. But he hit seven home runs in the final week of the regular season to give him 69 home runs going into the Millers' final game. His bid for 70 was denied when the Millers' final game was rained out.

In 1934, he picked up where he left off the previous September by hitting 17 home runs in the Millers' first 40 games. He was on a pace to hit 65 in his bid for a third season of at least 60 home runs. Despite missing three weeks in July with a knee injury, he had 33 home runs in 82 games and was still on his way to hit more than 60 home runs. Unfortunately, his season ended on July 29 when he suffered a fractured kneecap.

Hauser played for the Millers for two more seasons, hitting 23 home runs in 1935 and 34 in 1936.

All told, Hauser, who died in 1997 at the age of 98, hit 399 home runs in his minor league career. A plaque for him in the Wisconsin Athletic Hall of Fame reads "HR King of Minors."

A Truly International Series

The Junior World Series was a postseason playoff between the champions of the International League and the American Association. The Minneapolis

Millers competed in the series four times, but their last time—in 1959, their penultimate season in the American Association—was the most memorable.

The Millers, who were 95–67 during the regular season and managed by future big league manager Gene Mauch, won the American Association playoffs to advance to the series against the International League champion Havana Sugar Kings. The first three games of the best-of-seven series were scheduled for Met Stadium in Bloomington.

On September 27, the Sugar Kings won the series opener 5–2 before a crowd of 2486. The next day—a cool, windy Monday night—only 1065 fans showed up to watch the Millers win 6–5.

Game three, scheduled for an 8:15 PM start on Tuesday, September 29, was postponed because of the temperature: it was 47 degrees and the Sugar Kings, not used to the cool temperatures, had built fires in their dugout during the first two games of the series to stay warm. Officials from the two leagues decided that the rest of the series would be played in Havana. The island of Cuba, including its new political leader, Fidel Castro, was greatly interested in baseball and the series.

On Thursday, October 1, a crowd of 24,988 saw the Sugar Kings outlast the Millers 3–2 in 10 innings. The next day, Castro canceled a cabinet meeting so he could attend game four of the series. He saw the Sugar Kings prevail 3–1 in 11 innings.

On Saturday, with armed soldiers stationed in the dugouts and the stands in a show of power by Castro, the Millers won 4–2. The next day, the Millers won 5–3 to even the series at 3–3.

Game seven was rained out on Monday, October 5. The next day, a crowd of 20,000 saw the Sugar Kings rally from a 2–0 deficit after seven innings for a 3–2 series-winning victory.

The following season was the last for both the Millers and Sugar Kings. After the 1960 season, the Millers folded and the Sugar Kings were moved to New Jersey.

Pioneers

In 1946, Jackie Robinson broke the color barrier in organized baseball when he played for the Brooklyn Dodgers' Montreal farm team in the International League. Two years later, on May 22, 1948, Roy Campanella became the first African American to play in the American Association when he appeared in a game for the St. Paul Saints, who were also a Brooklyn Dodgers farm team. After 35 games with the Saints, Campanella was promoted to the Dodgers.

In June 1949, Ray Dandridge and Dave Barnhill became the first African Americans to play for the Millers. The 5-foot-7, 170-pound Dandridge, who had played professionally in Mexico, Cuba and the Negro Leagues, would spend four seasons with the Millers but would never reach the major leagues. In 1951, Dandridge, who had a career batting average of .331 in his 20-season career, was a roommate with future big-leaguer Willie Mays during Mays' brief stint with the Millers.

Dandridge, who has been called the best third baseman never to play in the major leagues, Campanella and Mays have been elected to the National Baseball Hall of Fame in Cooperstown, NY.

During their 59 seasons in the American Association, the Millers had 16 players and the Saints had six who eventually were named to the Hall of Fame. Among the Millers were Hoyt Wilhelm, Ted Williams and Carl Yastrzemski. Duke Snider is one of the former Saints in the Hall of Fame.

Hitting Machines

According to the Society for American Baseball Research (SABR), an estimated 165,000 players have appeared in a minor league baseball game (in 130 seasons through 2008).

The all-time leader in career hits in minor league baseball history is Duluth native Anthony "Spence" Harris. In 28 seasons—he appeared in 45 games at the age of 48—Harris had 3617 hits in 3258 games. He spent 10 seasons with the Minneapolis Millers, from 1928 to 1937.

Also according to SABR research, there have been only six hitting streaks of 49 consecutive games or longer in minor league history. Winnebago native Harry Chozen had a 49-game hitting streak for Mobile of the Southern Association in 1945.

A Good First Impression

Hall of Famer Lou Brock played just one season in the minor leagues before embarking on a 19-year major league career.

In 1961, Brock spent his first season in professional baseball with the St. Cloud Rox of the Class C Northern League. Brock, who had been named to the small-college All-America baseball team for Southern University, made quite an impression.

After getting three hits in his Rox debut, he hit safely in the team's first 14 games. On May 18, he went 4 for 5 with six RBI in a 14–3 victory over Grand Forks to extend his hitting streak to 15 games. His hitting streak ended the next day, but on May 20, he started a 10-game hitting streak. After the first month of the season, he was hitting .357.

Brock and the Rox finished strong. Over the final three weeks of the season, Brock put together an 18-game hitting streak (going 40-for-73 in the stretch). The Rox, meanwhile, put together the second-longest winning streak in league history. Between August 15 (the day before Brock started his latest hitting streak) and August 29, the Rox won 16 consecutive games. The streak was one shy of the Northern League record of 17, set by Eau Claire in 1942.

For the season, Brock batted a league-leading .361 and led in games played (128), runs scored (117), hits (181) and doubles (33). He also had 14 home runs, 82 RBI and 38 stolen bases.

Those numbers caught the attention of the Chicago Cubs, who recalled the 22-year-old outfielder, and Brock made his major league debut on September 10. By the time his 19-year MLB career was over, he had 3023 hits and had revolutionized the game with 938 stolen bases. The six-time All-Star also led the Cardinals to three NL and two World Series titles.

Other Rox of Note

Lou Brock was the third future Hall-of-Famer in a five-year span to play for the St. Cloud Rox.

In 1956, 18-year-old Orlando Cepeda won the Northern League Triple Crown with 26 home runs, 112 RBI and a .355 batting average in 125 games for the Rox. Cepeda was promoted to the Triple-A Minneapolis Millers the next season, and after hitting .309 with 25 home runs and 108 RBI in 1959, he went on to 17 years in the major leagues.

In 1958, Gaylord Perry, in his first season of professional baseball, went 9–5 with a 2.39 ERA for the Rox. Perry made his major league debut four years later, for the San Francisco Giants, and went on to win 314 games in his major league career.

Fun Is Good

The first version of the Northern League, a lower-level minor league, lasted until 1971; in 1993, it returned to the Midwest as an independent league.

Mike Veeck, the son of legendary MLB owner and promoter Bill Veeck, resurrected the "St. Paul Saints" name for one of the league's teams. Over the years, Mike Veeck and the Saints provided Minnesota baseball fans with inexpensive family fun (the team's motto is "Fun is Good") and some unforgettable moments.

Through the years, the Saints were a team with which former major league players (like Willie Aikens, Jack Morris and Darryl Strawberry) could try to prolong or restart their careers and future major leaguers (like J.D. Drew) could begin their professional careers.

An Equal-opportunity Employer

In 1997, Southern California native Ila Borders, the first female to receive a college baseball scholarship (at Southern California College), was invited to try out for the Saints.

Borders, a 5-foot-10 left-handed pitcher, was signed to a contract and on May 31, 1997, she made her debut for the Saints against the Sioux Falls Canaries in Sioux Falls, SD. In doing so, she became the first woman to appear in a regular-season minor league baseball game in the 20th century.

But Borders' stay with the Saints was brief: less than a month after her debut (and after just six innings pitched), she was traded to the Duluth-Superior Dukes. She would go on to become the first woman to be a starting pitcher in a men's professional baseball game and the first woman to be a winning pitcher in a men's professional game.

Like Father, Like Son

By providing former major leaguer Minnie Minoso with the chance for a couple of firsts, Mike Veeck continued a gesture started by his father.

Minoso had made his major league debut with the Cleveland Indians (owned by Bill Veeck) in 1949 and played in the major leagues until retiring in 1964 at the age of 42. In his major league career, he batted .300 at least eight times and had a career batting average of .298.

In 1976, Minoso became a four-decade player by appearing in three games for the Chicago White Sox (owned by Bill Veeck). Four years later, at the age of 58, he became a five-decade man by making two pinch-hitting appearances for the White Sox, who were still owned by Bill Veeck.

In 1993, Minoso had one at-bat for the St. Paul Saints (Mike Veeck's team) to become a six-decade player. Ten years later (in 2003), at the age of 81, Minoso batted once (drawing a walk) for the Saints to become a seven-decade player.

Women's Baseball

During World War II, Chicago Cubs owner Philip Wrigley was looking for ways to bolster attendance at major league baseball parks, and one of his ideas was the All-American Girls Professional Baseball League (AAGPBL). The AAGPBL started as a four-team league in 1943 and added two more teams the next year—one of which was in Minneapolis.

The team, which would play its home games at Nicollet Park (home of the Minneapolis Millers of the American Association), was called the Millerettes.

The team struggled, going 23–36 in the first half of the season; by mid-season, attendance was so low that it was decided that the team would play the rest of its games on the road. After the season, the team was relocated to Fort Wayne, IN.

Arguably, the Millerettes' best player was Helen Callaghan, who batted .287. Callaghan would eventually have a son, Casey Candaele, who would play in the major leagues. Another member of the Millerettes was Annabelle Lee, the aunt of future big league pitcher Bill Lee.

The league was the basis for the Hollywood movie *A League of Their Own*.

Two-sport Star

St. Paul native Jean Havlish played for the Fort Wayne Daisies of the AAGPBL in the early 1950s. After her baseball career was over, she had success in the sport of bowling. She won the Women's Minnesota State 600 Tournament four times and the state All-Events title twice, and in 1964, she became the first Minnesotan to win the Singles and All-Events titles at the Women's International Bowling Congress.

Havlish is a member of the Minnesota Sports Hall of Fame and the National Bowling Hall of Fame.

Toni Stone

Not many women have been honored with a display at the National Baseball Hall of Fame in Cooperstown, NY, but a Minnesota native named Toni Stone is one who has.

In 1937, at the age of 16, Stone began playing for a men's semi-professional baseball team—the Twin Cities Colored Giants.

In 1953, she became the first woman to play in the professional Negro Leagues when she signed with the Indianapolis Clowns of the Negro American League. She spent the 1954 season with the Kansas City Monarchs of the Negro American League. After her two-year stint in the Negro American League, she retired.

Stone, who is also a member of the Women's Sports Hall of Fame, died in 1996.

Kitten Ball

In 1887 in Chicago, about 50 years after the invention of baseball, the sport of softball was invented as an indoor sport.

Eight years later in Minnesota, a Minneapolis fireman named Lewis Rober created an outdoor version of softball to help keep his coworkers in shape. Rober's version was called "kitten ball," and the game quickly became popular across the United States.

In 1922, the name of the game was changed from kitten ball to "diamond ball." The term "softball" for the game wasn't used until 1926.

Bob Casey

From the Minnesota Twins' opening day in 1961 until 2004, the Twins had just one public address announcer—Bob Casey. Working more than 3400 Twins home games and countless other events, Casey is best remembered for several announcements including "no smoking in the Metrodome," his introduction of Kirby Puckett ("Now batting for the Twins, number thirty-four, Kiiiiiir-beeee Puckett!") and a strange announcement on August 25, 1970.

That night, during a Twins game against the Boston Red Sox, a bomb threat was called into Metropolitan Stadium and passed along to Casey to announce to the crowd. He said, "Your attention please. There will be an explosion in the stadium at 9:30 PM. I repeat, there will be an explosion!" There was a 40-minute delay in the game as security looked for a bomb. There was no explosion.

Minnesota Baseball Quick Facts

- Minnesota Twins former owner Calvin Griffith was a controversial owner and infamous for his insensitive racial comments. The most harmful of his comments came in 1978 during a Lions Club dinner speech in Waseca. When he tried to explain the reason for moving the Washington Senators to Minnesota in 1961, he said, "I'll tell you why we came to Minnesota. It was when we found out you only had 15,000 Blacks here. Black people don't go to ballgames, but they'll fill up a rassling ring and

put up such a chant it'll scare you to death. We came here because you've got good, hardworking white people here."
- In 1984, businessman Carl R. Pohlad bought the Minnesota Twins from Calvin Griffith. Before he purchased the team, it was rumored that if a local buyer for the Twins could not be found, the franchise would be relocated to Florida.
- The early 1980s were bad years for the Minnesota Twins and especially for pitcher Terry Felton. He played three games for the team during the 1980 season and lost all three. He was called back to the lineup in 1982 and went 0–13 over the season. Added to his three losses in 1980, it gave him the record for the most consecutive losses without a win.
- The Minnesota Twins won the club's first game over the New York Yankees by a score of 6–0.
- Between July 12, 2004 and May 1, 2005, Johan Santana of the Minnesota Twins put together the fourth-longest winning streak by an MLB pitcher since 1900. In that span, Santana was 17–0 with an ERA of 1.77.
- Every team needs a versatile player, but on September 22, 1968, Minnesota Twins' Cesar Tovar took that requirement to the extreme. Starting the game as the pitcher, Tovar moved behind the plate as catcher in the second inning, then from there moved to first base, then to second, shortstop, third base, left field, center field and finally to right field. Tovar was just the second player in major league history to

play all positions. The first was Athletics Bert Campaneris in September 1965.
- The Minnesota Twins are the only team in baseball history to record two triple plays in one game. On July 17, 1990, in a game against the Boston Red Sox, Gary Gaetti, Al Newman and Kent Hrbek combined to complete the plays in the fourth and eighth innings. The Sox won the game 1–0.
- Darn Minnesota weather can even cancel an indoor game. On April 14, 1983, a snowstorm caused the Twins' game versus the California Angels to be postponed. It was the only postponement in Metrodome history.
- Did you know that 28 former University of Minnesota Gophers have gone on to play in the major leagues?
- Kirby Puckett holds the Minnesota Twins' record for most career hits with 2304.
- The longest game in Twins history occurred on August 31, 1993, against the Cleveland Indians. The Twins won the game in the 22nd inning by a final score of 5–4. In total, the game lasted 6 hours and 17 minutes.
- In the history of the Baseball Hall of Fame, only three native Minnesotans have been inducted: Chief Bender (1953), Dave Winfield (2001) and Paul Molitor (2004).
- In 1988, the Minnesota Twins became the first AL team to pass the 3,000,000 mark in attendance during a single season.

- Did you know in the 12 home World Series games that the Minnesota Twins have played in, the only defeat came at the hands of Sandy Koufax, pitcher for the LA Dodgers?
- Rod Carew, infielder for the Minnesota Twins from 1967 to 1978, has won more batting titles than any other player in the AL, except for Ty Cobb.
- The Twins' Kirby Puckett became the first player to earn $3 million per season when he signed a contract before the 1989 season. Alex Rodriguez was signed for 27 million dollars in 2000. Babe Ruth made $50,000 in 1922.

Minnesota Baseball Quotables

"Now we know what sound feels like!"
 –Al Michaels, talking about the boisterous sounds of the Metrodome's crowd after the Twins won game seven of the 1987 World Series

"I was told I would never make it because I'm too short. Well, I'm still too short. It doesn't matter what your height is, it's what's in your heart."
 –Kirby Puckett

"There was no player I enjoyed playing against more than Kirby. He brought such joy to the game. He elevated the play of everyone around him."
 –Hall of Fame catcher Carlton Fisk

"In 1991, in playing against him in the World Series, if we had to lose and if one person basically was the reason, you never want to lose but you didn't mind it being (to) Kirby Puckett. When he made the catch and when he hit the home run, you could tell the whole thing had turned. His name just seemed to be synonymous with being a superstar."

–Atlanta Braves pitcher John Smoltz

"There must be a [heck] of a baseball game going on upstairs. And God must have needed a No. 3 hitter, because He took Puck way too soon."

–Kent Hrbek on former Twins teammate Kirby Puckett

"I like to look at magazines, read a few stories, read the captions. I don't like to socialize too much. You run into people who are not athletic-minded. They're bookworms or symphony patrons, and that's all they want to talk about."

–Minnesota Twins owner Calvin Griffith, about his wife's complaints that she missed the social and cultural life of Washington after he relocated the Washington Senators to Minneapolis. The couple eventually divorced

"I get a kick out of watching a team defense [sic] me. A player moves two steps in one direction and I hit it two steps in the other direction. It goes right by his glove and I laugh."

–Rod Carew, former infielder for the Minnesota Twins

"The worst thing is the day you realize you want to win more than the players do."

—Gene Mauch, former manager of the Minnesota Twins

"When I came up, you couldn't play if you couldn't bunt, but home runs have pretty much taken over the game today. You have to hit at least 25 homers to be a hero today. The game has changed so much. People want to see homers. Look around the league. Bunting has become a lost art. The baseball purists appreciate and respect Tony Gwynn and "Boggsie," but your batting average doesn't matter as much anymore. They want people who can put the ball over the fence."

—Kirby Puckett

"Hey, once in awhile, even a blind squirrel finds an acorn."

—Minnesota Twins catcher Tim Laudner, on his clutch performance in the 1987 playoffs against Detroit

"Losing streaks are funny. If you lose at the beginning, you are off to a bad start. If you lose in the middle of the season, you are in a slump. If you lose at the end, you're choking."

—Gene Mauch

"I don't think you'll find anybody here who will argue with you baseball wasn't meant to be played outdoors in the sunshine. I still believe that. But with the economics of the game of baseball today (in 1981), I think the majority of owners would prefer to have a stadium that would guarantee that they can get their 80 games in each year. Now we can stop worrying about the weather because when there is a game scheduled, we know we'll get it in."

> –Calvin Griffith, on the team's move to the covered Metrodome

"Calvin (Griffith), the wife is away. How about me coming to the ball game?"

> –Dwight D. Eisenhower to Calvin Griffith

"The team without (Harmon) Killebrew is like dressing up for a formal affair with a white tie and tails and then wearing muddy shoes."

> –Twins catcher Earl Battey

"Hitting is an art, but not an exact science."

> –Rod Carew, former Twins infielder

Chapter Three

The State of Hockey

The Capital of American Hockey

No other American state has produced as many NHL-level hockey players as Minnesota. Like their Canadian neighbors to the north, Minnesotans had long adopted the winter sport before many other states, and although they didn't have an NHL team until 1967, the culture of hockey had already worked itself into the lives of the people. It doesn't hurt to have plenty of snow and ice in the winter for kids to play on either, and as a result, many of those kids grew up to play hockey at the professional level.

But the title of greatest hockey city in Minnesota goes to the town of Eveleth, which has produced more hockey talent per capita than any other city. With a population of just 3865 after the 2000 census, it's hard to imagine this humble town as a breeding ground for professional hockey players, but over the generations, the good people of Eveleth have raised some quality players.

Legendary goaltender Frank Brimsek, winner of the 1939 Vezina Trophy and two-time winner of the Stanley Cup with the Boston Bruins in 1939 and 1941, was born in Eveleth in 1913; Mark Pavelich, of the Miracle on Ice team of the 1980s that won gold at the Lake Placid Olympics, was born in Eveleth in 1958; and father and son Sam and Pete Lopresti both credit the town of Eveleth as instilling in them the love of hockey.

If you ever visit the city, it's not hard to see its commitment to the game: the world's largest authentic hockey stick stands 107 feet tall in the small town, making it a landmark that's hard to miss. It's this passion for the game and the city's history of producing professional talent that led to the construction of the United States Hockey Hall of Fame in the town in 1973. The Hall of Fame has a beautiful display of the early years of hockey in the United States and memorabilia from the U.S. National Team's successes at the Olympics. Of course, Eveleth's native sons are not left out, as they receive their own special mention in the Hall.

The Creation of the Minnesota North Stars

When it was announced in 1965 that the NHL would be expanding from 6 to 12 teams, a partnership of nine businessmen, led by Walter Bush Jr., formed to seek a franchise for the Twin Cities. On February 9, 1966, NHL president Clarence Campbell announced that Minnesota, Oakland, Los Angeles,

Philadelphia, Pittsburgh and St. Louis would be awarded franchises.

Walter Bush Jr. appealed to the public for their help in naming the team, and of the 1536 entries received, it came down to five names: the Norsemen, the Voyageurs, the Blades, the Mustangs and the North Stars. On May 25, 1966, the new Minnesota North Stars were unveiled to the public. The name is derived from Minnesota's state motto, "L'Etoile du Nord," which means "The Star of the North" in French.

A few months after the naming of the team, a mad rush to complete the team's new arena began. It was a blessing the North Stars started on the road, as the construction crews had yet to finish the arena when the season began. Even by the home opener on October 21, 1967, crews were installing seats as fans arrived.

Despite a few bumps along the way, the North Stars got off to good start for an expansion club. They finished the season in fourth place in the Western Division and made it into the playoffs, where they reached the semifinals before being eliminated by the St. Louis Blues.

The Tragedy of Bill Masterton

Bill Masterton only played 38 games in the NHL, but his legacy would last forever. The Montreal Canadiens originally owned Bill Masterton's hockey rights, but they sold them to the Minnesota North Stars in June 1967, and Masterton was the first player signed by the North Stars.

The tough center's NHL career started off well when he scored the franchise's first goal on October 11, 1967. He wasn't one of the high-scoring players in the league, but his focus and dedication on the ice made him a perfect asset for the growth of a new franchise. It looked like he was headed for a long, successful career until the night of January 13, 1968, when the North Stars faced off against the Oakland Seals in Bloomington.

The game was going along smoothly, with both teams battling hard and getting equal chances on net. The North Stars started a rush up ice with Masterton leading the way, but as he came to the Seals' blue line, the puck slipped off his stick and passed between the two defensemen. As a helmetless Masterton rushed in between them to go for a breakaway, they collided awkwardly, sending him flying into the air. When he came down, he struck his head violently on the ice, knocking him unconscious. The play was stopped immediately as medics rushed out to tend to the fallen player. He was taken to hospital, but the damage to his brain was severe and the swelling could not be controlled. He eventually succumbed to his injuries and died in hospital two days later.

His career was short lived, but his legacy lived on: the NHL created the Bill Masterton Trophy the next year to be awarded to the player who best displays the qualities of perseverance, sportsmanship and dedication to the game of hockey. The first winner of the trophy was Claude Provost of the Montreal Canadiens.

Bookend Decades

1980–1981

Although the North Stars didn't have much in the way of postseason success, fans kept coming in the hopes that the team would eventually develop into a contender, but as the decade wore on, the North Stars' fate grew dim. From 1974 to 1979, the team made the playoffs only once and didn't even make it out of the preliminary round. As a result of the team's poor performance, fans stopped going to the games, and by 1979, the team was on the verge of folding operations completely.

However, just as things seemed doomed to fail, the North Stars saw the coming out of a young Bobby Smith, who won the Calder Trophy as the top rookie of the 1978–79 season. The team also saw the emergence of Steve Payne who, along with Al MacAdam, would lead the North Stars in scoring during the 1979–80 campaign with 42 goals.

The addition of some young talent energized the club and finally brought about some success on the ice. The 1979–80 season saw the return of the North Stars to the playoffs in 1980, and they made it all the way to the semifinals before being eliminated by the Philadelphia Flyers. The Stars had reasserted their position as one of the top teams in the league, but it was the arrival of a young rookie named Dino Ciccarelli that would propel the team deeper into the playoffs than they had ever been before.

Finishing the 1980–81 season in third place in the Adams Division put the North Stars in the playoffs for the second year in a row, but with a young lineup, the team was not expected to make it into the later rounds. But forwards Dino Ciccarelli and Steve Payne would, through sheer scoring power, help the team move all the way to the Stanley Cup final against the defending champion New York Islanders. Their opponents, however, were no pushovers, and the Islanders easily defeated the North Stars in five games.

It was a tough break for the Stars but an excellent sign for the future of the franchise. With the team's postseason success, fans began to return to the stadium to fill the seats and cheer on their team. But the euphoria would last only a handful of seasons before the team began to miss the playoffs in the late '80s, and talk once again turned to moving the franchise to another city.

1990–1991

The 1990–91 NHL season was by no means a success for the North Stars. They had to battle hard for every win, and by the end of the regular season, they had only scraped together 27 victories and 39 losses. But, by some miracle of hockey statistics, the Stars made the final playoff spot in their division and had a second chance to prove to their fans that they could be a factor in the NHL.

It wasn't going to be easy, as the first team they faced was the league-leading Chicago Blackhawks and the Vezina-winning goaltending of Ed Belfour. But, with some timely saves from goaltender Jon Casey and the veteran presence of Bobby Smith and Brian Propp, the Stars defeated the Blackhawks in six games and went on to make their second trip to the Stanley Cup finals in a decade.

The run to the finals brought much-needed life and revenue back into the North Stars franchise, but their Cinderella run would end there. They faced the Pittsburgh Penguins, who proved too deep in scoring talent, and the Stars simply could not put enough goals in the net to match.

In the final game, the Penguins handed the Stars the most lopsided loss in the Stanley Cup finals since 1905 by beating them 8–0. It was an embarrassing way for the Stars to finish off their magical run, and it would ultimately be their last appearance in the Stanley Cup finals.

An Auspicious Debut

In their first season in the NHL, the Minnesota North Stars came within one goal of advancing to the Stanley Cup Finals.

The North Stars were coached by Wren Blair, who also served as the team's general manager. Blair had a reputation for recognizing talent: while working for the Boston Bruins, he signed a 14-year-old Canadian junior player (and future Hall of Famer) named Bobby Orr to a contract.

In the first round of the playoffs, the North Stars, who had finished fourth in the West Division with a 27–32–15 record and 69 points, took on the Los Angeles Kings. The North Stars lost the first two games (both played in Los Angeles) of the best-of-seven series, but they regrouped to win the next two games in Bloomington.

The Kings won the next game in Los Angeles to take a 3–2 series lead, but the North Stars rallied to win game six 4–3 on Milan Marcetta's goal in overtime. In the series' deciding game, in Los Angeles, the North Stars pounded the Kings and future Hall of Fame goaltender Terry Sawchuk 9–4.

In the next round, the North Stars met the St. Louis Blues. The series had controversy before it even started. An oversight by the North Stars' front office cost the team a home game in the upcoming series. The team shared their home, Met Center, with the Minnesota Muskies of the ABA; inexplicably, North Stars officials forgot to reserve dates for home playoff games, so, the team was forced to play five of the seven games against the Blues in St. Louis.

The Blues won the series opener in St. Louis 5–3. The next night in Bloomington, the North Stars evened the series with a 3–2 overtime victory. They then won game three in St. Louis 5–1 to take a 2–1 lead in the series.

Game four of the series, which should have been played in Minnesota, was played in St. Louis and won by the Blues, 4–3, in overtime. The Blues then took a 3–2 lead in the series by winning game five in St. Louis, 3–2, in overtime.

The series returned to Minnesota, where the North Stars tied the series with a 5–1 victory. But the Blues prevailed two nights later in St. Louis, winning the seventh game 2–1 on a goal by Ron Schock at 2:50 of the second overtime.

Farewell, North Stars

The early 1990s were hard times for some markets in the NHL, as the realities of big city business began to hurt the NHL franchises located in smaller markets such as Quebec, Winnipeg and, Minnesota. The NHL would be going through a major update in the next decade, with teams across the league in the planning stages of modernizing their stadiums to accommodate more fans and more revenue-winning luxury boxes and corporate seats. Those franchises that could not provide the housing and fans to put into the seats would fall to the wayside. Add to that a struggling team on the ice, and it was a certain recipe for a franchise to fold. By the 1992–93 season, North Stars team owner Norman Green announced that he could no longer operate the team in a market that had been losing money since 1985. Minnesota was going to lose their beloved North Stars to the city of Dallas.

When asked by reporters about the move after playing in the final game in North Stars history, forward Bobby Smith said, "A good part of my career has been spent in Minnesota, and the fans know how I feel about them. They've always been there, both for me and the team."

The new Dallas Stars franchise made its debut in the Lone Star State for the 1993–94 season, while the Met Center sat empty. It was an especially bitter pill to swallow when, during the 1999 playoffs, the Dallas Stars made it all the way to the Stanley Cup finals and won, but the knowledge that NHL hockey would indeed return to Minnesota helped to ease the pain.

Return to the Wild

The effort to return NHL hockey to the Twin Cities began the moment the final buzzer sounded at the end of the North Stars' 1993 game seven playoff defeat, their last game as a Minnesota team. Only four years later, on June 25, 1997, the NHL announced that Minnesota Sports & Entertainment, a limited partnership formed by Bob Naegele Jr., had won the rights to open a franchise back in the great state of Minnesota, with 2000–01 as their opening season.

The appeal was put out to the public to send in their best ideas for a name for the Minnesota team. After going through thousands of submissions, it came down to just six: the Blue Ox, the Freeze, the Northern Lights, the White Bears, the Voyageurs and the Wild. The name of the Minnesota Wild was unveiled to the public along with the logo of a wild animal that appears to look like a wild cat or, to some, a bear, with the silhouette of a forest, a setting sun and a red sky. The Wild have never specified what animal is on the logo, as the design is more about symbols of the state and the hockey team. The mouth of the wild animal resembles one of Minnesota's many rivers and its eye doubles as a star in the sky, in homage to the North Stars.

"We think it best represents what Minnesota hockey fans hold most dear," said the newly named chief executive officer of the new team, Jac Sperling.

Former player Doug Risebrough was named general manager, and the process of constructing a new team began. A new stadium called the Xcel Energy Center would be built on the site of the former Saint Paul Civic Center in St. Paul. Jacques Lemaire was named the team's first coach, and the team's future superstar, Marian Gaborik, was selected third overall by the Wild at the 2000 NHL Entry Draft. Gaborik would score the first goal in Wild history at their debut game on October 6, 2000.

Since the opening game until the time of writing, the Minnesota Wild have had some good years and some bad. They have hovered just above the basement of the league and have pushed into the later rounds of the playoffs, but they still have not managed to gain the ultimate prize. Some fans can console themselves with the fact that they had invested something in their former North Stars that had gone on to win the Cup in 1999, but the real Wild fans will never be satisfied until the Cup comes home to "L'Etoile du Nord."

Ciccarelli in his Birthday Suit

Minnesota North Star forward Dino Ciccarelli had just come off one of his best seasons with the club in 1986–87. The tenacious forward was not blessed with great size or the skills of Wayne Gretzky, but he would place himself in front of the opponent's net, take the punishment from the defensemen and get rewarded with plenty of goals from that spot. It took a lot of hard work, and after a game or season ended, Ciccarelli liked to walk around his house nude or semi-nude.

One morning when he ventured out of his house to retrieve the newspaper, he forgot to put on his pants and ended up giving the neighbors a little more than they bargained for while they sipped their coffees. One of the shocked neighbors called the police, and Ciccarelli was charged with indecent exposure. He pled guilty and served 50 hours of community service for his minor indiscretion.

Ciccarelli, who retired following the 1998–99 season, played 19 seasons in the NHL, scoring 608 goals (17th most in league history). Going into the 2010–11 season, he ranks 45th on the NHL's all-time scoring list with 1200 points. Ciccarelli was inducted into the Hockey Hall of Fame in 2010.

Marian Gaborik's Five

On December 20, 2007, the Minnesota Wild welcomed the New York Rangers to town on a chilly Saturday night in St. Paul. The Rangers seemed to have been affected by the weather, as not a single player on the team could mount a resistance to the talent of Marian Gaborik on that night.

The New York Rangers were the first to score, but Gaborik struck first with a natural hat trick—two of the goals scored in the span of 1 minute and 51 seconds. The crowd tossed their baseball caps and wool hats onto the ice in celebration, but Gaborik wasn't done.

The Wild got another goal, but the Rangers responded with two of their own to put the score at 4–3 for Minnesota. Gaborik came to the rescue of his teammates and scored the go-ahead goal in the third period to make it four goals for Gaborik. Less than two minutes later, Gaborik scored his fifth and final goal of the night on a crowd-pleasing breakaway. The game ended 6–3; Gaborik was named the game's first star and received thunderous applause from the fans.

"When the crowd yelled during his last shift and stood up and were clapping, I just had a flash, '[Hall of Famer Guy] Lafleur,'" coach Jacques Lemaire said.

Said Rangers forward Brendan Shanahan, "We ran into a world-class hockey player who had the game of his life. I've seen a lot of him, and he's maybe one of the top three or four players in the game as far as being dangerous with the puck."

Gaborik had registered the franchise's first five-goal game and became the NHL's first player to do so since Detroit's Sergei Fedorov scored five goals against the Washington Capitals on December 26, 1996.

"First goes in, second goes in, you feel good, confident," Gaborik said. "It just gets you going and going."

Gone Too Soon

Sergei Zholtok came to the Minnesota Wild from the Edmonton Oilers in 2001 and found a comfortable spot on the team as a second- and third-line center. He had never been a star on the ice, but his hockey sense was tuned and he could be counted on in the defensive zone. He was a fan favorite in Minnesota for three seasons until he was traded to the Nashville Predators in 2004. Although his stay with the Wild was brief, he had made many good friends: Darby Hendrikson even followed him to play for the HK Riga 2000 of the Belarusian Extraliga during the NHL lockout of 2004–05.

During a game between Riga 2000 and HC Dinamo Minsk on November 3, 2004, Zholtok left the game with five minutes remaining and collapsed in the dressing room. The first to his side was Hendrickson, who called for help and did what he could for his friend, but was ultimately helpless to save him as Zholtok slipped away in his arms. An autopsy determined that the cause of death was heart failure resulting from a cardiac arrhythmia. This, unfortunately, was not the first time Zholtok had experienced the cardiac problems: in January 2003, he was forced to leave a game due to this same arrhythmia and ended up missing seven games.

"I was really honored to have him on the team," said an emotional Riga 2000 president Viesturs Kozioles. "He was a patriot for his country and for hockey who never took a shift off and always devoted time to trying to make our young players better."

Zholtok scored 111 goals and had 147 assists during his 12-year NHL career. He had a career-best 26 goals for the Canadiens in 1999–00.

Streak Busters

During the 1979–80 season, the Philadelphia Flyers put together a 35-game unbeaten streak. The streak, which included 25 victories and 10 ties, is the longest in major league sports history. On January 7, 1980, the streak ended in Bloomington, in a 7–1 loss to the Minnesota North Stars.

Doubling the Fun

Major league professional hockey came to Minnesota in 1967 when the NHL expanded by six teams (the first change in the league's makeup since 1942).

Five years later, a second professional hockey team arrived in the Twin Cities when the Minnesota Fighting Saints became one of the 12 charter franchises of the World Hockey Association (WHA). The Fighting Saints called downtown St. Paul home—first playing in the old St. Paul Auditorium while the St. Paul Civic Center was being built next door—and began play in the 1972–73 season.

By their fourth season in St. Paul, the Fighting Saints had serious financial problems and wouldn't complete the season; they folded on February 27, 1976. But St. Paul wouldn't be without professional hockey for long.

Following the 1975–76 season, the Cleveland Crusaders of the WHA were squeezed out of Cleveland when the California Seals of the NHL relocated there and became the Cleveland Barons. Ironically, both the Crusaders and the Barons would eventually find homes in Minnesota.

The Crusaders, after considering a move to Florida, relocated to St. Paul in July 1976 and became the "new" Minnesota Fighting Saints. But the reincarnation of the Saints lasted less than a season, and the team folded on January 17, 1977.

The WHA lasted just two more seasons before four of the league's franchises—Edmonton, New England (Hartford), Quebec and Winnipeg—joined the NHL.

The Barons, meanwhile, lasted just two seasons in Cleveland. Following the 1977–78 season, they were merged with the Minnesota North Stars.

Never Dull

During their five seasons in St. Paul, the Fighting Saints lived up to their name.

During the 1974–75 season, Gord Gallant of the Fighting Saints led the WHA in penalty minutes with 203, while teammate Ron Busniuk was third in the league with 176.

The Saints, who finished third in the Western Division with 87 points, opened the 1975 playoffs with a 6–5 victory over the New England Whalers. Following the game, Gallant got into a fight with Saints coach

Harry Neale and was immediately suspended by the team. He was traded to Quebec following the season.

The next season, Gallant was third in the league with 297 penalty minutes.

MacNaughton Cup

In 1916, the St. Paul Athletic Club team—which included future U.S. Hockey Hall of Fame members Moose Goheen and Nick Kahler—won the MacNaughton Cup, awarded to the top team in the American Amateur Hockey Association. The St. Paul team also shared the Cup in 1920 with the Canadian Soo and reached the finals in 1922 and 1923.

The MacNaughton Cup was given to the top amateur team until 1932 and is now used by the Western Collegiate Hockey Association.

Godfather of Minnesota Hockey

After playing football and hockey for the University of Minnesota—he was a member of the Gophers' 1939–40 hockey team that was named the national champion by the Amateur Athletic Union (AAU)—Eveleth native John Mariucci signed a contract with the Chicago Blackhawks of the NHL. At the time, there were few Americans playing in the league.

After just 17 games with the Blackhawks' Providence farm team, Mariucci joined the Blackhawks. He appeared in 23 games with the team in the 1940–41 season and 47 games in the 1941–42 season before joining the coast guard.

Following three years in the coast guard, Mariucci returned to the Blackhawks in 1945. He spent the next three seasons with the team before spending the final three seasons of his playing career in the minor leagues (one season each with St. Louis of the AHL and St. Paul and Minneapolis of the United States Hockey League (USHL).

In 1952, Mariucci became the hockey coach at the University of Minnesota. In 14 seasons, he coached the Gophers to a 215–150–15 record. He took a leave from the Gophers position to coach the 1956 U.S. Olympic team.

After coaching the Gophers, Mariucci went to work for the expansion Minnesota North Stars as an assistant general manager. He is a member of both the U.S. Hockey Hall of Fame and the Hockey Hall of Fame.

Herb Brooks

In a state that has hockey legends like Moose Goheen, Ching Johnson, John Mariucci and John Mayasich, Herb Brooks is special to Minnesota hockey fans.

Brooks, a St. Paul native, played for the University of Minnesota hockey team from 1956 to 1959. He was the last player cut from the 1960 U.S. Olympic team (which won the gold medal) before playing for the 1964 and 1968 U.S. Olympic teams.

In 1972, Brooks was hired to revive the Gophers hockey program, which was coming off an 8–24 season (the worst winning percentage in the program's history) in 1971–72. It took him just two seasons to turn the program around. The Gophers went 15–16–3 in his first season. In his second season, the Gophers finished second in the WCHA during the regular season and then won the playoffs to earn a spot in the National Collegiate Athletic Association (NCAA) Final Four.

The Gophers edged Boston University 5–4 in the semifinals and then defeated WCHA rival Michigan Tech 4–2 in the championship game to earn the first NCAA hockey title in school history. They were the first team in 25 years to win the NCAA title with a roster made up solely of Americans.

The Gophers and Michigan Tech would play for the NCAA championship in each of the next two seasons, as well. Michigan Tech won the rematch in 1975, 6–1. The Gophers defeated Michigan 6–4 in the 1976 championship game to claim their second national title.

In 1979, the Gophers earned their third NCAA title in seven seasons under Brooks, defeating North Dakota 4–3 in the championship game. Following that season, Brooks took a leave of absence to coach the U.S. Olympic Team to the gold medal at the 1980 Olympics in Lake Placid, NY.

Instead of returning to the University of Minnesota following the 1980 Olympics, Brooks accepted an NHL coaching position with the New York Rangers.

Straight to the NHL

In his one season of high school hockey, Phil Housely had 31 goals and 34 assists in 22 games for South St. Paul High School.

Following that 1981–82 season, Housely was selected in the first round (the sixth player taken overall) of the NHL draft by the Buffalo Sabres. The 5-foot-10 defenseman went straight to the NHL and would stay for 21 seasons.

When he retired following the 2002–03 season, he was the NHL's all-time leader in points scored by an American-born player. In 1495 games, he scored 1232 points (338 goals and 894 assists).

Following his retirement as a player, he returned to Minnesota to coach high school hockey.

NHL Draft Milestones

The NHL began its draft in 1962, but it was 17 years before a U.S. college hockey player would be selected in the first round. In 1979, the Buffalo Sabres selected University of Minnesota defenseman Mike Ramsey with the 11th overall pick.

After the NHL began allowing 18-year-olds to be selected in the draft, the first U.S. high school player drafted was Jay North of Bloomington Jefferson High School. North was the 62nd player selected in the 1980 draft.

In 1983, the Minnesota North Stars had the No. 1 pick in the NHL draft and they selected Brian Lawton.

Lawton was the first American-born player to be taken first overall in the NHL draft.

Hockeytown, USA

Warroad, a town of 1600 in northwestern Minnesota, near the Canadian border, calls itself "Hockeytown, USA." It's hard to argue with the label—the town has produced at least six players who have won a gold medal in Olympic hockey.

Two of the gold medalists are brothers Billy and Roger Christian, who helped lead the U.S. Olympic team to the gold medal at the 1960 Olympics. After the Olympics, the Christian brothers returned to their hometown of Warroad, where they founded a company that manufactured hockey sticks. Billy's son, Dave Christian, was a member of the 1980 Olympic team that won the gold medal in Lake Placid.

Another Warroad citizen has played a prominent role in hockey in Minnesota: Cal Marvin, the youngest of five sons of lumber baron George Marvin, founded a senior amateur hockey team called the Warroad Lakers. The Lakers, perennially one of the top amateur teams in the country, has won the Allan Cup (senior hockey's equivalent to the Stanley Cup) several times. Marvin is the member of four Halls of Fame, including the U.S. Hockey Hall of Fame.

A General Says No to Augsburg

In January 1928, the AAU's Ice Hockey Committee was considering four college hockey teams to represent the United States at the 1928 Olympics in St. Moritz, Switzerland.

The committee selected the team from Augsburg, a small private college in Minneapolis with an enrollment of 300, to represent the U.S. Augsburg was chosen over another Minnesota team—Eveleth Junior College—and two teams from Boston—Harvard and the University Club of Boston.

For the team to make the trip to Switzerland, Augsburg needed to raise $4500, half of the cost of sending the team to Europe, in just two weeks. The school reached the fundraising goal, but several days before the team was to leave for Switzerland, the U.S. Olympic Committee (USOC) overruled the AAU, deciding that the U.S. would not send a hockey team to Switzerland.

The chairman of the USOC—Major General Douglas D. MacArthur (yes, that General MacArthur)—reportedly felt the Augsburg team "was not representative of American hockey." The Augsburg team's lineup included five Hansen brothers, who were raised in Canada before moving to Minneapolis.

Minnesota and the Olympics

The first time the U.S. fielded an Olympic hockey team was at the 1920 games in Antwerp, Belgium. The U.S. team, which included four members of the St. Paul Athletic Club team, won a silver medal.

In 1952, seven players with Minnesota connections helped the U.S. earn a silver medal at the Oslo Games. Four years later, seven Minnesotans—including future governor Wendell Anderson—were members of the U.S. team, which won a silver medal at Cortina d'Ampezzo, Italy. The team was coached by Minnesotan John Mariucci.

At Squaw Valley in 1960 the U.S. team, with eight Minnesotans, defeated Russia in the semifinals and then Czechoslovakia for the gold medal.

Ten Minnesotans were members of the 1972 team, which won a silver medal.

In 1980, Minnesotan Herb Brooks coached the U.S. team, which included 12 Minnesotans on its 20-man roster, to the gold medal. En route to the medal, the U.S. upset Russia 4–3 in the semifinals. It was the first Olympic loss in 12 years for the Russians, who had won five of the previous six Olympic hockey gold medals, dating to 1956. The victory over the Russians was dubbed the "Miracle on Ice." Just two weeks before the Olympics, the U.S. team had lost to the Russians 10–3 in an exhibition game. The Russians had also tuned up for the Olympics by defeating a team of NHL all-stars. *Sports Illustrated* called the U.S. victory over Russia the "greatest sports moment of the 20th century." In the gold medal game, the U.S. defeated Finland 4–2.

Notables

Natalie Darwitz was a hockey legend in Minnesota before she was even in high school. As a seventh-grader, she scored 85 goals for the Eagan High School girls' hockey team, and at the age of 15 she was named to the U.S. Women's National Team. Darwitz went on to play for the University of Minnesota and the U.S. Olympic team.

Ivan "Ching" Johnson played for the minor league Eveleth Rangers and the Minneapolis Millers before signing with the New York Rangers of the NHL in 1926. He went on to play 12 seasons in the NHL and was an NHL All-Star in 1932 and 1933.

Willard Ikola is another Eveleth product to have had a huge impact on Minnesota hockey. After high school, Ikola was a two-time All-America goalie for the University of Michigan and a member of the 1956 U.S. Olympic team. After his playing career, he became a high school coach, leading Edina High School to a 616–149–38 record and eight state championships in 33 seasons.

R.H. "Bob" Peters coached the University of North Dakota hockey team for two seasons before taking over the Bemidji State hockey program in 1965. Over the next 35 seasons as the Beavers coach, Peters guided the team to 13 small-college national hockey titles while becoming the first U.S. college hockey coach to win 700 games at one school. At the time of his retirement in 2001, his 744 career victories ranked second highest in the nation.

The mentor for many of the Eveleth products was Cliff Thompson. Thompson led Eveleth High School to 12 consecutive appearances in the state high school hockey tournament (1945–56) and four consecutive state championships (1948–51). During that period, Eveleth had a 78-game winning streak.

Thompson retired in 1958 with a 534–26–9 record (a .946 winning percentage).

Girls' Hockey

Hockey in Minnesota dates to the 1890s. The University of Minnesota played its first hockey game in 1895—eight years before the first game was played in Eveleth.

Boys' high school hockey dates to the 1920s, and the first official boys' state tournament was played in 1945.

By the late 1980s, interest in hockey by girls was steadily rising. In the fall of 1993, eight high schools in the state fielded girls' hockey teams, concluding the season in February 1994 with a tournament.

Several weeks after the tournament, Minnesota became the first state to sanction girls' hockey as a varsity sport for high school girls.

That November, the first official girls' hockey season in Minnesota began with 24 varsity teams, culminating in February 1995 with a four-team state tournament.

In 2010, there were 124 girls' high school hockey teams in the state.

Minnesota Hockey Quick Facts

- As of the 2010–2011 season, Mike Modano is the last member of the Minnesota North Stars still active in the NHL. The 40-year old Modano, in his 21st NHL season, is No. 1 in NHL history in goals and points by an American-born player. Going into the 2010–11 season, he had 557 goals and 1359 points. Currently

playing for the Detroit Red Wings, he had two goals and six assists in 20 games before suffering a wrist injury, which required surgery.
- The following are some NHL players born in Minnesota: Andrew Alberts, Minneapolis; David Backes, Minneapolis; Mike Antonovich, Calumet; Neal Broten, Roseau; and Paul Holmgren, St. Paul.
- Marian Gaborik holds the Wild team record for the most goals and points in one season with 42 goals and 83 points during the 2007–08 season.
- In 2002–03, Minnesota Wild head coach Jacques Lemaire won the Jack Adams Trophy for the best coach of the season.
- The first Minnesota North Star to win the Bill Masterton Trophy was Al MacAdam for the 1979–80 NHL season.
- Wayne Connelly led the Minnesota North Stars in scoring during their first season, with 35 goals and 21 assists. He became the first player in NHL playoff history to score on a penalty shot when he scored in the North Stars' 7–5 victory over the Los Angeles Kings in Bloomington in 1968—the fourth penalty shot in the NHL playoffs, and the first in 24 years.
- During their 26 seasons in Minnesota, the North Stars had a revolving door for head coaches. A grand total of 15 head coaches were employed, and several of them more than once. Only 16 of the 26 seasons saw a North Stars coach lead the team the entire season.

Minnesota Hockey Quotables

"I've been thinking about this for a long time, but it's still an unbelievable disappointment to go out this way. I don't like to be known as a loser, but in the Minnesota North Stars' last season, that's exactly what we were."

–North Star veteran Neal Broten, after losing game seven of the Division semifinals against the Detroit Red Wings in the 1993 playoffs. It would also be the final game of the North Stars franchise

"Shades of Pavel Bure. It was just like watching Bure in the day. I mean, Gabby was banking them in out of the air, scoring on breakaways, skating through everybody, making highlight-film goals. My God, he was doing it every which way tonight."

–Wild forward Mark Parrish, a former teammate of Bure's, speaking of his Wild teammate Marian Gaborik's five goal night on December 20, 2007, against the New York Rangers

"That was a Minnesota (Wild) type of game, where they laid back in the neutral zone. Those aren't the most exciting games to watch and certainly not the most exciting to play. But we played into their hands at times, turning the puck over, instead of getting it deep."

–Detroit Red Wings defenseman Mathieu Schneider after a frustrating game against the Wild's defensive system

Chapter Four

On the Court

The NBA's First Dynasty

Few know this, but before becoming the Los Angeles Lakers of legend, the franchise was located thousands of miles to the northeast in beautiful Minneapolis. The Lakers actually got their start as the Detroit Gems of the National Basketball League (NBL) in 1946, but after a 4–40 record over the season and horrible financial returns, owner C. Boring sold the team to businessmen Ben Berger and Morris Chalfen. The two partners moved the team and changed the name to the fabled Lakers, chosen in reference to Minnesota's nickname, "the Land of 10,000 Lakes." The Minneapolis Lakers were born and would play at the Minneapolis Auditorium and the Minneapolis Armory at the start of the 1947 season.

The new Lakers were lucky the team had failed in Detroit, because their miserable 1946 season meant that the team had the first overall selection at the Professional Basketball League of America dispersal draft. They used this selection to sign the legendary George

Mikan. As a result of having one of the most dynamic centers of the times and an infusion of players from the University of Minnesota, the Lakers won the NBL championship in their first season.

For the 1948 season, the Lakers transferred over to the competing Basketball Association of America (BAA) and won that championship, as well. As if that wasn't enough, they continued their domination when the BAA and the NBL joined to form the National Basketball Association (NBA) by winning a third consecutive championship.

They won the NBA championship again in 1949 and 1950, were eliminated in 1951 but went on to win another three straight championships (1952, 1953 and 1954), making them the most successful expansion franchise in sports history. However, the party could not last for Laker fans, and the team began to lose its core players to retirement and trades and could not compete with other emerging powerhouses like the Boston Celtics. By the end of the 1958 season, the Lakers finished with a 19–53 record and as a result, attendance began to fall rapidly. Even the team's resurgence in 1959 and a trip into the finals against the Boston Celtics could not bring people back into the seats.

Prior to the 1960 season, the Minneapolis Lakers' then-owner Bob Short packed up and moved the franchise to Los Angeles. The team was not renamed, despite the fact that Southern California has a distinct lack of their geographical namesake.

Minneapolis would not see another NBA franchise until the debut of the Minnesota Timberwolves in 1989.

Minneapolis Lakers versus the Globetrotters

In the late '40s and into the '50s, the NBA looked nothing like its modern version. There were only a few teams in the league, and its fan base was still in its infancy. The Minneapolis Lakers were one of the more successful franchises, drawing well at home, but when they traveled to the big city of New York the games would draw only around 6000 people.

This lack of support in certain regions meant that team owners constantly looked for new ways to promote the game. It was around the same time that an annual basketball tournament held in Chicago was played, involving all professional teams from the NBA, the NBL and two all-black teams from New York—the New York Rens and the Harlem Globetrotters.

The Globetrotters today put on a show rather than a sporting event, but back in the 1940s and early 1950s they were a serious basketball team with some of the best professional players of the time, including Sonny Boswell, Sweetwater Clifton and Marques Haynes. Globetrotters owner Abe Saperstein thought it would be a good idea for the Lakers and the Globetrotters, being the best teams at the time, to play each other.

The two teams played for the first time in February 1948 in Chicago, with the Globetrotters beating the Lakers by two points. The formula was a complete success; the two teams played a high-paced, athletic display of basketball that attracted huge sellout crowds. The game was such a hit financially that it was decided that the Lakers and the Globetrotters should play every year. When the annual games came to the Minneapolis auditorium, people would line up at three in the morning just for a chance at grabbing a ticket. In all, the teams played each other seven times between 1948 and 1952, with the Lakers winning five of the games. The two teams played against each other one last time in 1958, and the Lakers won that game.

The Dynasty Comes to an End

On April 12, 1954, the Minneapolis Lakers defeated the Syracuse Nationals 87–80 to claim their sixth league title in seven seasons.

The next day, the Lakers were the guests of honor at a luncheon at a downtown Minneapolis hotel. The *Minneapolis Tribune* reported that NBA president Maurice Podoloff told the crowd, "one can only deal with superlatives in discussing this team. I will say that it is the greatest team in the history of basketball and deserves a place not earned by any other team in any type of athletics. The Lakers have been the greatest contributing factor to the success of the NBA. The record of the Minneapolis Lakers—winning six world titles in seven years—will remain unchallenged for years to come."

The league title was the last for the NBA's first dynasty. Following the season, Lakers star George

Mikan retired (although he briefly returned to play 37 games in the 1955–56 season). The Lakers did have a winning record (40–32) in the 1954–55 season and reached the second round of the playoffs, but that was their last winning season during their stay in Minnesota.

Optimism and Despair

The Lakers had an NBA-worst 19–53 record during the 1957–58 season and missed the playoffs for the only time in their 13 seasons in Minnesota.

Led by rookie Elgin Baylor, the team's fortunes began to improve in the 1958–59 season. Baylor averaged 24.9 points (fourth best in the league) and 15.0 rebounds (third best in the league) per game, leading the Lakers to a 33–39 record and second place in the NBA's Western Division. Baylor also scooped up the league's Rookie-of-the-Year honors.

Returning to the playoffs, the Lakers won a first-round best-of-three series against the Detroit Pistons to advance to the West Division finals against the St. Louis Hawks.

The Hawks, who were led by Bob Pettit (the league's top scorer with a 29.2 points-per-game average) and were second best in the league, defeated the Lakers 124–90 in the series opener in St. Louis. The next night, in Minneapolis, the Lakers regrouped and pulled out a 106–98 victory to even the series.

The Hawks looked impressive in game three, winning 127–97, but the rest of the series belonged to the

Lakers as they defeated the Hawks three consecutive times to win the series 4–2 and advance to the NBA finals for the first time in five years.

The Celtics, with future Hall of Famers Bill Russell (who led the league in rebounding by averaging an incredible 23 rebounds per game), Bob Cousy and Bill Sharman, swept the Lakers 4–0 to win their second NBA title in three seasons. With the title, the Celtics started the league's second dynasty. The championship was the first of eight consecutive for the team.

Lucky Landing for the Lakers

On January 17, 1960, the Lakers lost a Sunday afternoon game in St. Louis to the Hawks, 135–119. The day only got worse for the Lakers. Following the game, the team headed to the airport for the return flight to Minneapolis, but their charter flight was delayed for several hours because of an ice storm.

Around 8:30 PM, the team's plane (a DC-3 that had been used during World War II as a cargo plane) took off. Shortly after the plane was in the air, its generators failed, causing it to lose its electrical system and radio.

Pilot Vern Ullman, a retired U.S. Marine who had flown in both World War II and the Korean War, tried to take the plane above the clouds to navigate by the stars. After five hours and with no way to tell how much fuel the plane had left, Ullman decided to land the plane in a snow-covered corn field near Carroll, Iowa. None of the 23 on board was injured.

The Final Season

Despite the improvement on the court, the Lakers went into the 1959–60 season with serious questions about the team's future in the state.

They flew to the west coast where they played two games—one in San Francisco and one in Los Angeles—against the Philadelphia Warriors and Wilt Chamberlain. The receipts from the two games (and the trade of Larry Foust to St. Louis for three players and $10,000) helped the financially strapped team meet their payroll obligations.

The team finished the regular season with a 25–50 record (in third place in the West) and then surprised the second-place Detroit Pistons to advance to the division finals. In the West Division finals, the Lakers would face their old nemesis, the St. Louis Hawks.

The Lakers won games two, four and five to take a 3–2 lead and move within one victory of a return trip to the NBA finals. But the Hawks won game six in Minneapolis 117–96 to tie the series. On Saturday, March 26, the Hawks outlasted the Lakers 97–86 in St. Louis to win the series.

One month later, Lakers owner Bob Short announced he had reached a tentative agreement to move the franchise to Los Angeles, but the NBA didn't initially approve the deal. Concerned about increased travel costs for the league's teams, the league's owners voted 7–1 against the deal on April 27.

Moments after the vote, the owners learned that Abe Saperstein (of Harlem Globetrotters fame) had announced he was forming a league, which would begin play later that year. Saperstein said that among the cities in which the league would field teams were Los Angeles and San Francisco. Now concerned about losing Los Angeles to a rival league, the NBA owners reconvened and re-voted. The second vote was unanimous in favor of allowing the Lakers' move to Los Angeles.

Short, a trucking tycoon who had become the Lakers' president by virtue of being the lead investor in a group of 100 investors, eventually sold the Lakers to Jack Kent Cooke for $5 million.

The Lakers weren't the only franchise that Short moved. In 1968, Short purchased the Washington Senators for $9 million. Just three years later, he moved the team to Arlington, TX.

Replacing the Lakers

Following the Lakers' departure for the west coast in 1960, it would be 29 years before another NBA franchise would call Minnesota home. But, just seven years after the Lakers left, professional basketball returned to Minnesota and it was former Lakers great George Mikan who played a prominent role in the return.

In February 1967, another league decided it wanted to challenge the NBA (Abe Saperstein's American Basketball League had been short-lived) and the American Basketball Association (ABA) announced it would begin play in the fall of 1967. Mikan, who was running a travel agency in Minneapolis, agreed to become the league's new commissioner, and the league awarded one of its 10 franchises to Minnesota.

The team, named the Minnesota Muskies, would share the new Met Center in Bloomington (across the parking lot from Met Stadium) with another expansion team, the Minnesota North Stars of the NHL. The teams played their first home games one day apart—the North Stars on October 22 and the Muskies on October 23.

The Muskies were one of the new league's top teams, but they struggled financially from the start. Led by Mel Daniels, who was named the league's rookie of the year, the team compiled a 50–28 regular-season record and finished second in the East Division. They reached the second round of the playoffs, where their season ended with a loss by the eventual champion, the Pittsburgh Pipers.

Just one month after their season ended, the Muskies' owners—citing low attendance (the team had averaged just 2500 fans per game) and claiming losses of $400,000—announced they were moving the franchise to Miami.

Minnesota didn't have to wait long before getting another pro basketball team. In June, about a month after the Muskies had left town, Minneapolis businessman William J. Erickson announced he had purchased the Pittsburgh Pipers and moved them to Minnesota. Despite winning the league title and having one of the league's top players (Connie Hawkins), the team had lost a reported $250,000 in its inaugural season.

The team was renamed the Minnesota Pipers. Former Hamline University and Lakers star Vern Mikkelsen was named the team's general manager and Jim Harding was named the coach. By coincidence, the Pipers' first regular-season game in Minnesota was against the team they had replaced. In front of a crowd of only 1943, the Pipers defeated the Miami Floridians (originally the Minnesota Muskies) 126–94.

It was a rocky season for the Pipers in Minnesota. Injuries limited Hawkins to just 47 games, but when he was healthy, he was outstanding. In a span of nine days early in the season, he had games of 57 points and 53 points.

Harding was fired at midseason after getting into a fight with Gabe Rubin (who was still a minority owner of the team after selling 85 percent of the club to Erickson) at the league's All-Star game in Louisville.

Struggling to draw fans in the Twin Cities, the team played eight games in Duluth (about 150 miles north of the Twin Cities) in a hope to create a regional fan base. The regular season ended the way it had a started—in front of a small crowd. Only 1345 fans showed up for the Pipers' final regular-season home game.

Not long after the season, the team, which had lost $400,000 during the season, announced it was moving back to Pittsburgh.

The Return of the NBA

George Mikan played a crucial role in the return of the NBA to the area. In 1984, Minnesota Governor Rudy Perpich formed a task force, whose mission was to convince the NBA to put an expansion team in the state. Mikan was named to lead the task force.

Mikan and the group worked for more than a year on the presentation they would make to the league's expansion committee. On April 3, 1987, the committee listened to the group's presentation and recommended to the league's board of directors that Minnesota should be awarded an NBA franchise.

On April 22, 1987, the NBA's board of directors voted unanimously to expand by four teams—awarding franchises to Charlotte, Miami, Minnesota and Orlando. Charlotte and Miami would begin play in 1988, while Minnesota and Orlando would begin 1989.

What's In a Name?

In 1947, a group of Minneapolis businessmen purchased the Detroit Gems of the NBL and moved the franchise to Minneapolis.

After the team's arrival in Minnesota, a local radio station ran a contest to choose the name of the new team. While the contest was going on, Max Winter, the team's general manager, reportedly decided he wanted to call the team the Minnesota Vikings. The radio station running the contest heard of Winter's idea and convinced him it would be bad public relations for him and the team if the contest wasn't legitimate.

On October 2, 1947, the *Minneapolis Times* reported that the team would be called the Minneapolis Lakers. A Minneapolis resident received a $100 savings bond for being the first to suggest "Lakers" as the team's name.

Thirteen years later, Winter, who had left the Lakers to concentrate on securing a pro football franchise for Minnesota, was part of the Minnesota group that was granted an NFL expansion team. He was finally able to use his "Vikings" nickname.

Forty-one years after the contest to name the Lakers, another Minnesota team needed a nickname. A statewide poll of 842 city councils was conducted to name the NBA expansion franchise. The name "Timberwolves" was selected by a 2-to-1 margin over the next popular suggestion, "Polars."

Marv and Harv

After being turned down in their bid to buy the Minnesota Twins, Marv Wolfenson and Harvey Ratner decided to pursue an NBA franchise. The two men, who owned a chain of health clubs, made bids for the Milwaukee Bucks and the Utah Jazz, but both franchises were eventually sold to a local buyer.

After the failed bids, the two men joined the effort to bring an NBA expansion team to the state, and in April 1987, they were awarded an NBA franchise (the expansion fee was $32.5 million). While the team was playing its first season in the Metrodome, Ratner and Wolfenson were having a new arena built.

From the outset, the new arena was a financial burden for the two men and within five years, the financial problems almost caused the pair to move the franchise.

While the arena was under construction, the institution that had backed the arena's financing—Midwest Federal Savings and Loan—had its own money problems and the financing fell apart. To finish the arena, Ratner and Wolfenson had to refinance at higher interest rates. The arena was completed, but it cost $15 million more than originally planned.

With their health club chain also going through tough financial times, Ratner and Wolfenson struggled with the debt tied to the construction of their new arena.

By early 1994, during the team's fifth season in Minnesota, the only solution for the pair's financial problems was to sell the franchise and the arena. The Minnesota legislature approved a public buyout of the arena, making it seem that the state would avoid losing the Timberwolves just two years after the Minnesota North Stars had relocated to Dallas.

But sixteen days after the state-approved buyout of the arena was announced, Ratner and Wolfenson announced they had reached an agreement to sell the franchise to a group that intended to move the team to New Orleans. However, the NBA vetoed the deal and the men started looking for a local buyer.

Three months later, they announced they had reached an agreement to sell the team to Minnesotan

Glen Taylor. The sale price was $88.5 million—well below the bid of $152.5 million by the New Orleans group (which had included boxing promoter Bob Arum). Ratner and Wolfenson were able to recoup some of the difference several months later when the city of Minneapolis announced it would take ownership of the arena for $54 million.

East Bay Funk

In each of their first five years of existence, the Minnesota Timberwolves had a selection among the top 10 overall picks in the annual NBA draft. In their fifth draft (in 1993), the team selected University of Nevada at Las Vegas guard Isaiah "J.R." Rider with the fifth-overall pick. Rider would spend three memorable seasons with the Timberwolves.

One of the highlights of Rider's stay in Minnesota came during his rookie season. In 1994, the Timberwolves played host to the NBA All-Star game. The team, who had won just 19 games in 1992–93 and would win just 20 in the 1993–94 season, didn't have a player selected to play in the All-Star game. But Rider represented the team in the slam-dunk contest, which was part of the weekend's festivities.

Rider won the contest with a dunk he had perfected in his hometown of Oakland, California, called the "East Bay Funk."

Rider averaged 16.6 points per game during his rookie season. In his second season with the Timberwolves, he averaged 20.4 points per game (just one of five Timberwolves to average 20 points per game for a season). In his third season, he averaged 19.6 points per game.

While talented on the floor, his off-court behavior got more attention. The team fined him on numerous occasions for skipping practice and missing team flights. He was convicted of first-degree assault after kicking the female manager of a suburban sports bar. He was also arrested in his hometown for possession of illegal cell phones.

The final straw likely came after an on-court incident late his third season with the team. After being ejected from a game, Rider refused to leave the floor. He finally left after his mother left her courtside seat, went on the court and convinced her son to go to the locker room.

Following the season, the Timberwolves traded Rider to Portland.

Joe Smith

In the summer of 1995, 20-year-old Joe Smith, a 6-foot-10 forward who had played two seasons at the University of Maryland, was the first player selected in the NBA draft (by Golden State).

Midway through his third season, Smith was traded by Golden State to the Philadelphia 76ers. After averaging a respectable 13.3 points and 8.1 rebounds per game in his first three seasons in the league, he became a free agent after completing the season with Philadelphia.

In January 1999 (the 1998–99 season didn't begin until February 5 because of a labor dispute between the league and players), Smith signed a multi-year contract with the Timberwolves. In the shortened season, he averaged 13.7 points and 8.2 rebounds per game. In his second season with the Timberwolves (1999–2000), he averaged 9.9 points and 6.2 rebounds per game.

Just days before the start of the 2000–01 season, the NBA announced that the contract Smith had signed with the Timberwolves two years earlier violated the league's collective bargaining agreement. The contract had been reported to the league as a three-year contract when the two parties had actually agreed to seven years, so because the team didn't report the actual deal, it was seen to have violated the league's salary cap rules. The league voided the contract, making Smith a free agent, and levied harsh sanctions against the franchise. The franchise was fined $3.5 million and ordered to forfeit its first-round draft pick for the next five years (two of the first-round picks—in 2003 and 2005—were later restored to the team).

Smith signed with the Detroit Pistons, but returned to the Timberwolves following the 2000–01 season. He spent two seasons with the Timberwolves before being traded to Milwaukee.

In his three seasons with the Timberwolves, he averaged 10.3 points per game.

Malik Sealy

On the same day that the Timberwolves first signed Joe Smith, they also signed free agent Malik Sealy.

Sealy, a 6-foot-8 guard and forward who had played collegiately at St. John's (NY), averaged 8.1 points per game in 33 games in his shortened first season with the Timberwolves. In his second season with the team, he started 61 games and averaged 11.3 points and 4.3 rebounds per game.

Shortly after that season, in the early morning hours of May 20, 2000, Sealy was killed in a car accident in St. Louis Park. He was on his way home after attending a birthday party for teammate Kevin Garnett when his vehicle was hit by a drunk driver going the wrong way down a divided highway.

His jersey number (No. 2) was the first one retired by the Timberwolves.

Latrell Sprewell

In the summer of 2003, the Timberwolves acquired Latrell Sprewell from the New York Knicks in a deal involving four teams. As part of the trade, Minnesota sent Terrell Brandon to Atlanta and Mark Jackson to Philadelphia.

The acquisition of Sprewell, a four-time NBA All-Star, was controversial, but owner Glen Taylor and general manager Kevin McHale thought the talented forward was worth the risk.

Sprewell, a former first-round draft choice by Golden State, had his stint with the Warriors marred by a suspension for what NBA Commissioner David Stern called the "premeditated assault" of Warriors coach P.J. Carlesimo.

During a practice on December 1, 1997, Sprewell put his hands around Carlesimo's neck and threatened to kill him. Moments later, Sprewell punched the coach. Two days later, the Warriors terminated Sprewell's $32-million contract and the day after that Stern suspended the player for one year—the longest suspension in league history not related to drugs.

In March 1998, an arbitrator ruled the suspension was "excessive punishment" and re-instated Sprewell's contract. The suspension, which was reduced to 68 games, cost him $6.4 million.

In his first season with the Timberwolves, Sprewell helped lead the team to a franchise-record 58 victories and their first-ever playoff series victory. Still, the season wasn't without controversy. In December 2003, playing his first game in New York since the trade, Sprewell was given a technical foul for swearing at the Knicks bench. The next day, he was fined $25,000 by the league.

The Timberwolves eventually reached the Western Conference Finals, where their season was ended by the Los Angeles Lakers, 4–2.

Coming off the best season in franchise history, Timberwolves management had reason to be optimistic about the 2004–05 season. However, the optimism was quickly overshadowed by turmoil.

During training camp, Sprewell, who was under contract for $14 million for the upcoming season, said he wanted an extension. He issued a deadline of November 3 (opening day of the season) for the team to extend his contract. If the team didn't extend his contract before the deadline, he wanted to be traded.

"Why should I help them win a title," he told the *Minneapolis Star Tribune*. "I got my family to feed."

Early in the season, in a game in Los Angeles, Sprewell made a vulgar remark to a fan. He was suspended for one game by the league for the incident.

He became an unrestricted free agent after the season.

Trading a Superstar

During the 1999–2000 season—the season before the NBA's sanctions—the Timberwolves compiled a 50-32 record, the first 50-victory season in team history. They slipped to 47-35 in 2000–01 but improved in each of the next three seasons. But the lack of first-round draft picks and the Sprewell affair started a decline of the franchise. With their fortunes on the court and attendance slipping, the Timberwolves decided to trade the top player in franchise history.

On July 31, 2007, the Timberwolves traded 10-time All-Star Kevin Garnett to the Boston Celtics for five players (Al Jefferson, Gerald Green, Ryan Gomes, Theo Ratliff and Sebastian Telfair) and two first-round draft picks.

The 31-year old Garnett had just finished his 12th season with the team. In 927 regular-season games, he averaged 20.5 points and 11.3 rebounds per game. In 47 career playoff games, he averaged 22.3 points and 13.4 rebounds.

An Idea Before its Time

For the first seven years of the 1970s, the only opportunities for women to play professional basketball were in Europe.

That changed in 1978, when the Women's Professional Basketball League (WPBL) was formed. League founder Bill Byrne, who had helped found the World Football League, hoped the league would be able to take advantage of the interest in women's basketball sparked by the 1976 Olympics (the first time women's basketball was an Olympic sport).

One of the league's eight franchises was granted to a Minnesota group, which was headed by Gordon Nevers, a funeral home operator. The team, named the Minnesota Fillies, got off to a promising start in July 1978 by selecting Trish Roberts, a University of Tennessee star who had been a member of the 1976 U.S. Olympic team, in the league's first player draft.

In their first game, the Fillies lost to the Iowa Cornets before a crowd of 4102 at the Met Center. They finished their first season in third place in the league's Midwest Division with a 17–17 record, but missed the playoffs.

Their second season was a success on the court as they won 22 of 34 regular-season games and reached the semifinals of the league's playoffs.

Their third season didn't go well on the court or financially. The Fillies, who moved their games from suburban Bloomington to the Minneapolis Auditorium, won just 7 of 36 games and faced a player boycott late in the season after the team owners missed a payroll.

The rest of the league was struggling too. The WPBL had hoped to continue to build on the interest generated by the Olympics, but the U.S. boycott of the 1980 Olympics hurt its chances. The league folded after the 1980–81 season.

Let's Try This Again

After the demise of the WPBL in 1981, it would be at least 10 years before another attempt at establishing women's professional basketball in the U.S.

In 1993, the Women's Basketball Association was formed. Two years later, the league relocated an Indiana franchise to Minnesota for the 1995 season. The team, led by former University of Minnesota standout Molly Tadich, lasted just one season.

Finally, in the spring of 1997, the NBA announced the formation of the Women's National Basketball Association (WNBA) and said the new league—which would play in the summer—would be owned by the NBA and its owners.

In April 1998, the WNBA announced it would expand by two teams for the 1999 season—adding teams in Minnesota and Orlando. Each franchise had to meet the league's condition of pledges for 5000 season tickets.

Katie Smith, who had played at Ohio State and on the 1998 U.S. National team that won gold at the World Championships, was allocated to the Minnesota franchise—named the Lynx—by the league. She was reunited with Lynx coach Brian Agler, who had coached her for three seasons with Columbus of the ABL, and three of her Columbus teammates.

On June 12, 1999, the Lynx made its WNBA debut with a 68–51 victory over the Detroit Shock before a crowd of 12,222 at the Target Center.

Smith was the star of the franchise for its first six and a half seasons. On July 13, 2005, Smith, who was in her 11th professional season, became the first woman to score at least 5000 points in a professional U.S. career. Less than three weeks later, the Lynx traded her to the Detroit Shock for two players and a first-round draft choice.

Minnesota Basketball Quick Facts

- In August 1992, Mannie Jackson, a senior vice president for the Minneapolis-based Honeywell Corp., purchased the Harlem Globetrotters to become the first African American to own a major sports franchise. Jackson played for the Globetrotters from 1962 to 1964.
- The Timberwolves' first season was played at the Metrodome while their unique building, the Target

Center, was under construction. The Metrodome was constructed originally for football and baseball games, usually selling out 50,000 seats on a regular basis. Basketball-specific stadiums in the NBA in the late 1980s normally had seating capacities of 25,000–35,000 seats. Because of the number of available seats at the Metrodome, the Timberwolves set several attendance records, including highest exhibition game attendance at 35,156 and an opening game attendance of 35,427. Even though they won only 22 games that season, they averaged 26,160 fans per home game and became the first team in NBA history to draw more than one million fans for a season. The Target Center seats 20,500 for a basketball game.

- Former Timberwolves star Kevin Garnett, at just 19 years of age, became the first player in 20 years to be drafted into the NBA straight out of high school.
- Garnett was also a member of the gold medal–winning USA Men's Basketball team at the 2000 Olympic Games.
- In their first 21 seasons in the NBA (the 2010–11 season was their 22nd), the Minnesota Timberwolves won just two playoff series (both in 2004). In eight postseason appearances, the Timberwolves have a 17–30 record.
- Since joining the NBA in 1989, the Minnesota Timberwolves have had 10 coaches. Only one—Flip Saunders—has coached longer than two seasons.

- The first African American to play basketball for the University of Minnesota was future Pro Football Hall of Famer Bobby Bell. Bell appeared in three games during the 1960–61 season after joining the team at midseason.

Minnesota Basketball Quotatables

"We have to do the impossible, but it is possible."
–Kevin Garnett

"I guess I've done just about everything in life people told me I wasn't able to do.... I respond pretty well to somebody telling me there's something I can't do. I started wearing glasses when I was 12, and people told me then that anyone who wore glasses could never be a great athlete. And I always took a lot of taunts because I was so big. I was always being challenged as a kid, but I grew stronger, and (the taunts) stopped pretty fast. In college, they laughed and said I'd trip over the foul line. After a while, that stopped too. I guess you could say I've always had a burning desire to be successful. I still do."
–Minneapolis Lakers legend George Mikan

"Is he (Kevin Garnett) a franchise player? I can't say that. But this kid does some things that excite you."
–Minnesota Timberwolves coach Bill Blair after the team had drafted Garnett

"We must face the facts that the Lakers did not have a fair chance here. They were denied suitable facilities. It has been nobody's fault, only a case of the town lacking suitable facilities. On a comparison of facilities alone, the move is justified."
—Minneapolis Tribune columnist Dick Cullum, regarding the Minneapolis Lakers' move to Los Angeles

"I had tears in my eyes before the game started. It was great to see all those fans.... We couldn't have written a better script for our first home game."
—Minnesota Lynx guard Tonya Edwards, after Lynx defeated the Detroit Shock 68–51 in their first WNBA home game

Chapter Five

On Campus

Doctor on Campus

The University of Minnesota played its first football game in 1882, but the sport didn't attract much attention for the school until the arrival of Dr. Henry Williams in the fall of 1900. Williams, who had been an All-American football player at Yale and was a graduate of the University of Pennsylvania Medical School, was the first full-time football coach at Minnesota.

Besides being able to give his players their annual physical, Williams was also a pretty good coach. In his first three seasons as the Gophers coach, they went 28–3–4. Additionally, he was innovative and would eventually fill an important role on the college football rules committee. He was the first to propose legislation legalizing the forward pass (early college football had resembled rugby) and in 1906, the forward pass was legalized.

Trophy Time

In 1903, the Gophers gained national attention by winning their first 10 games by a combined score of 506–6. Their 11th game—against the University of Michigan in Minneapolis—would bring them more attention.

Michigan, coached by Fielding H. Yost, was 7–0 in 1903 and riding a 29-game winning streak going into the game. During the streak, the Wolverines had outscored their opponents 1631–12 (including 447–0 in 1903) to earn themselves the nickname "Point-a-minute Wolverines" and their coach the nickname "Hurry Up" Yost.

More than 20,000 people packed Northrop Field for the 2:30 PM kickoff to see if the Gophers could end a four-game losing streak to the Wolverines.

With just a couple of minutes remaining in the game, the Wolverines appeared to be on the verge of extending their winning streak over the Gophers with a hard-fought 6–0 victory. But the Gophers scored to tie the game—the first touchdown of the season allowed by the Wolverines—and some Minnesota fans were so thrilled by the touchdown that they rushed the field. The final two minutes of the game were called off and the game ended in a 6–6 tie.

The game would eventually become known for more than the end of Michigan's winning streak: it was the birth of one of the most famous rivalry trophies in college football history.

As they left the field in the bedlam, the Wolverines left behind a water jug, which was found the next day by a University of Minnesota equipment man. When he got back to Michigan, Yost wired Minnesota athletic director L.J. Cooke to return the jug, but Cooke wired back that the Wolverines would have to win their jug.

The teams didn't play again until 1909, when the Wolverines won back their jug. Since then, the teams have played for the "Little Brown Jug" 91 times. Michigan leads the series, 66–22–3.

That's a Lot of Points

The Gophers opened the 1904 season on September 17 with a 107–0 victory over a high school team. The 107 points were five shy of the school record of 112 (set the previous season in a 112–0 victory over Macalester) and 21 shy of "the world's record for scoring" held by Michigan, which had established the record in 1901 in a 128–0 victory over Buffalo.

A little over a month later, both the Gophers and Michigan would break the record.

On October 22, Michigan defeated West Virginia 130–0 to surpass its scoring record. The same afternoon, the Gophers faced Grinnell (of Iowa), a team they had defeated 102–0 two years earlier. The Gophers, who brought a 7–0 record into the game and had not allowed a point (outscoring their opponents 438–0), defeated Grinnell 146–0 to break Michigan's record. The Gophers' 146 point-performance would stand for nearly 13 seasons until Oklahoma defeated Kingfisher College 179–0 in 1916.

One week after routing Grinnell, the Gophers defeated Nebraska 16–12. The 12 points were the only points allowed by the Gophers that season. They finished the season 13–0 (outscoring their opponents 725–12) to extend their unbeaten streak to 28 games, the tie against Michigan the previous season the only blemish on their streak.

The Gophers won their first seven games in 1905 to extend their unbeaten streak to 35 games. That streak, the longest in the school's history, came to an end in a 16–12 loss to Wisconsin. In Dr. Henry Williams' first six seasons as Gophers coach, they went 65–4–5.

Between 1933 and 1936, under coach Bernie Bierman, the Gophers would put together the second-longest unbeaten streak in school history—a 30-game unbeaten streak, which included 21 consecutive victories in one stretch and four ties.

Trophies, Part Two

The football rivalry between the University of Minnesota and the University of Wisconsin is so old, it's gone through two trophies. Starting in 1930, the winner of the game was awarded the "Slab of Bacon" Trophy.

In 1945, Wisconsin defeated the Gophers 26–12 in Minneapolis. The Badgers returned to Madison with the trophy, but it was apparently misplaced. When the Gophers won the next year in Madison, they were told the trophy couldn't be located.

So, in 1948, the teams replaced the lost trophy with a new one—Paul Bunyan's Axe—and have played for it every year since.

In 1994, the missing trophy was found in a storeroom at Wisconsin's Camp Randall football stadium. Considering that it had been "missing" since 1945, Wisconsin officials couldn't explain how the score of every game in the series between 1930 and 1970 was printed on the back of the trophy.

Another Trophy Story

When the University of Minnesota and the University of Iowa football teams closed out the 2010 regular season in Minneapolis, it was the 104th meeting between the two. The rivalry, which began in 1891, has been carried forward every year since 1931.

In 1934, the Gophers defeated the Hawkeyes 48–12 in Iowa City. The victory was part of an undefeated season for the Gophers, who were named the National Champions after the season (the first of five national championships in an eight-year span). After the game, several Iowa newspapers accused the Gophers of intentionally trying to hurt Hawkeyes running back Oz Simmons, who had to leave the game because of an injury.

The day before the teams' rematch in Iowa City in 1935, Iowa Governor Clyde Herring created a controversy by telling a reporter, "If the officials stand for any rough tactics like Minnesota used last year, I'm sure the crowd won't."

Gophers coach Bernie Bierman was stunned by the comments and thought they were inflammatory. He asked for extra police protection for his team. Some parents of Minnesota players wanted Minnesota Governor Floyd Olson to call out the National Guard to protect the Gophers.

Olson defused the escalating situation by sending a telegram to Herring. In the telegram, he offered to wager a prize hog over the game's outcome.

The game was played without incident, and the Gophers rallied from a 7–0 halftime deficit for a 13–7 victory. A few days later, Herring, who said his original comments had been misconstrued, delivered a pig to Olson's office in St. Paul. The pig was named "Floyd."

A likeness of the pig was sculpted into a bronze statue. Since 1936, the trophy, dubbed "Floyd of Rosedale," has been awarded to the winner of the annual game.

Gino Cappelletti

After playing football for the University of Minnesota, Keewatin native Gino Cappelletti played for several teams in Canada before finally getting the chance to play professional football in America. He signed with the Boston Patriots of the AFL in 1960.

Cappelletti, who played 10 seasons for the Patriots, was one of just three players who played in every game of the AFL's 10-year existence (1960–69). Both a receiver and a kicker, he is the all-time leading scorer in AFL history and is in the AFL's all-time top-10 in receiving yards and receptions. He led the AFL in scoring five times and was named the MVP of the AFL in 1964. In his AFL career, he kicked 176 field goals; during his college career with the Gophers, he kicked just one field goal.

A Football Casualty

The Gophers and Iowa State met in football every year but one between 1895 and 1915. The Gophers dominated the series, winning 18 of 20 games (including 16 consecutively between 1899 and 1915).

The teams took a break in the series for seven years before resuming the rivalry in Minneapolis in 1923.

On October 6, 1923, the Gophers opened their season with a 20–17 victory over Iowa State, which had opened its season the previous week. Iowa State halfback Jack Trice had left the game with an injury and did not return; following the game, Trice accompanied the team back to Ames, IA. The next day, however, he began having difficulty breathing. Less than 48 hours after the game, he died from internal bleeding.

The teams did play again the next season—playing to a 7–7 tie in Minneapolis—but that was the last meeting between the two for 65 years.

Iowa State's football stadium is named after Jack Trice.

William "Pudge" Heffelfinger

In 1887, the University of Minnesota football team needed one more player for a game and recruited a high school senior named William "Pudge" Heffelfinger to play.

After graduating from Minneapolis Central High School, Heffelfinger went on to enroll at Yale, where he was a three-time All-America from 1889 to 1991.

In 1892, he became the first "professional" football player when he was paid $500 to play for the Allegheny (PA) Athletic Association in a game against its rival, the Pittsburgh Athletic Club. He paid dividends for Allegheny: he forced a fumble, recovered it and returned it for the game-winning touchdown.

After coaching at the University of California for one season in 1893, Heffelfinger returned to Minneapolis. He coached the Gophers football team to a 7–3 record in 1895 but then started a long, successful career in business and politics (serving as a Hennepin County Commissioner).

Bobby Marshall

Minneapolis Central High School product Bobby Marshall is one of the top all-around athletes in state history. He played three sports—baseball, football and track—at the University of Minnesota, lettering in football for the Gophers from 1904 to 1906.

Following the 1906 season, Marshall, who was an end, was named first-team all-conference—the first African American to hold that title in the conference that would become known as the Big Ten.

After earning a law degree from the University, he briefly coached football before playing professional baseball for the Chicago Leland Giants of the Negro Leagues and professional football for the Minneapolis Marines and the Duluth Kelleys.

Marshall was still playing semi-professional baseball past his 50th birthday. He died in 1958 at the age of 78. In 1971, he was elected to the National Football Foundation Hall of Fame.

Paul, Babe and Bronko

One of the endearing legends in Minnesota history is that of Paul Bunyan and Babe, his blue ox. Another is the one of Bronko Nagurski.

After becoming the Gophers' football coach in 1925, Dr. Clarence Spears was on a recruiting trip in Northern Minnesota. Legend has it that when he stopped to ask a farmer for directions, the farmer—an 18-year-old named Bronko Nagurski—picked up the plow he was using and pointed Spears in the right direction. Spears had found a football player.

After joining the Gophers in 1927, Nagurski continued to add to his legend. In 1928, he added new meaning to the phrase "playing hurt." In the Gophers' 6–0 victory at Wisconsin, he played wearing a steel corset to protect his ribs and spine for an injury later described as two broken vertebrae.

In 1929, Nagurski became the first and only player to be named an All-America at two positions (fullback and defensive line) in the same season.

Following his Gophers career, he played for the Chicago Bears of the NFL for eight seasons before retiring after the 1937 season. Six years later, he returned for one more season and helped lead the Bears to the NFL title.

In December 1999, *Sports Illustrated* named Nagurski Minnesota's top athlete of the 20th century. His name lives on with the Nagurski Trophy, which is awarded annually to college football's top defensive player.

Coaching Legends

The state of Minnesota and the Gophers football program have produced several college football coaching legends.

Bud Wilkinson, who had been a first-team All-America for the Gophers in 1935, coached the University of Oklahoma to 47 consecutive victories, a winning streak that spanned the 1953–57 seasons. Wilkinson coached the Sooners to a 145–29–4 record and three national titles (1950, 1955 and 1956) in 17 seasons.

Grant, a three-sport letterman for the Gophers, played in the NBA, the NFL and the CFL before beginning his coaching career with Winnipeg of the CFL. In 1967, he became the coach of the Minnesota Vikings.In a 28-year coaching career, his teams won 290 games and he was the first person to be elected to both the Pro Football Hall of Fame and the CFL Hall of Fame.

John Gagliardi, another Minnesota coaching legend, was still active in 2010. In 1953, St. John's University hired Gagliardi, who had coached the previous four seasons at Carroll College (MT), to replace Johnny "Blood" McNally as the Johnnies' coach. The 2010 season was his 58th at St. John's and 62nd as a college coach. Gagliardi, the winningest coach in college football history (478 victories), is the first active coach to be named to the College Football Hall of Fame. The Johnnies went 7–3 in 2010, giving him a 478–129–11 career record. In 2006, he surpassed Amos Alonzo Stagg, who coached the University of Chicago and Pacific for 57 seasons (from 1890 to 1946), for the most seasons as a college coach.

Fulfilling a Father's Vow

In 1941, Bruce Smith of the Gophers became the only player in the school's history to win the Heisman Trophy, awarded annually since 1935 to the top college football player.

Smith's storied football career actually started 30 years earlier. Smith's father, Lucius, played for the Gophers football team in 1910 and 1911. In 1910, after the Gophers suffered a 6–0 loss to Michigan, a disappointed Lucius Smith reportedly vowed that one day he would have a son who would beat Michigan.

In 1941, Faribault native Bruce Smith led the Gophers to an 8–0 record, a victory over Michigan, a Big Ten title and their fifth national championship in eight seasons. Even though he was only third on the team in rushing yards, Smith outpolled Notre Dame's Angelo Bertelli and Stanford's Frankie Albert to win the award.

Smith enlisted in the Navy in 1942 and, following World War II, played in the NFL for four seasons.

Heisman Trophy

Several other Gophers have also placed high in Heisman voting. The year before Smith won the award, George "Sonny" Franck was third in the voting. Paul Giel fell short in the voting two times, finishing third in 1952 and second in 1953. In 1960, Tom Brown was second, and in 1961, Sandy Stephens was fourth. Bobby Bell was third in 1962.

The oldest athlete to win the trophy in its 75-year history was Minnesotan Chris Weinke. He played high school football for Cretin-Derham Hall and then six years of professional baseball with the Toronto Blue Jays before enrolling at Florida State. In 2000, at the age of 28, he won the Heisman Trophy.

In 2003, another Minnesota high school product finished high in the voting. University of Pittsburgh and current NFL receiver Larry Fitzgerald Jr., who played for the Academy of Holy Angels (in suburban Richfield), was second in the voting.

Golden Days of the Little Brown Jug Series

In the long history of the Little Brown Jug, the Gophers have had only two stretches where they dominated Michigan. The first was between 1934 and 1942 when the Gophers won nine consecutive games. The only other time the team won more than two consecutive games against the Wolverines was when they won four consecutive games between 1960 and 1963.

So, there's a good chance that only a few former Gophers can make the claim that Bill Daley can. During his four-year college football career, Daley never played for the losing team in the series. That alone makes him rare. What makes him unique is that he played for both teams.

Daley, a Melrose native, joined the Gophers as a freshman in the fall of 1940, and he and the team defeated Michigan 7–6 en route to a national championship. The next season, he played a key role—rushing for 50 yards and intercepting a pass—in the Gophers' 7–0 victory over the Wolverines in Ann Arbor.

In 1942, Daley and the Gophers defeated Michigan 16–14 in Minneapolis for their ninth consecutive victory in the series. Following the season, he enlisted in the Navy, and in 1943 he was stationed near the University of Michigan campus. Former Gophers coach Fritz Crisler, now the Michigan coach, convinced Daley to play his senior season for the Wolverines.

On October 23, 1943, the Wolverines—with Daley and Elroy "Crazy Legs" Hirsch—defeated the Gophers 49–6. After the season, Daley, who had been a first-team All-Big Ten selection for the Gophers in 1941, was named an All-America.

Withstanding the Heat

Murray Warmath, who had been an assistant to two legendary college football coaches—Tennessee's Robert Neyland and Army's Earl Blaik—became the University of Minnesota football coach in 1954. He had initial success as the Gophers coach, leading them to a 16–9–2 record in his first three seasons. The Gophers went into Warmath's fourth season (1957) ranked No. 6 in the nation and, after opening the season with three consecutive victories, moved up to No. 3.

But over the final seven weeks of the 1957 season, the Gophers won just once. In 1958, they went 1–8 and in 1959, they were 2–7. Following the 1959 season, Warmath was hung in effigy outside a campus dormitory and reportedly had garbage dumped on his lawn.

In 1960, fortunes improved for the team. They opened the season with seven consecutive victories—matching their combined victory total of the previous three seasons—and were named the national champion following the end of the regular season. Following the regular season, they played in the Rose Bowl, their first bowl-game appearance in school history. The Gophers lost to Washington, 17–7.

The Gophers returned to the Rose Bowl following the 1961 season and defeated UCLA 21–3. Warmath coached the team through the 1971 season.

Expanding the Recruiting Area

The struggles of the Gophers football team in 1957, 1958 and 1959 led many people in Minnesota to call for Warmath's dismissal as coach.

But Warmath survived the tough times and restored the program to prominence primarily because of his simple decision to expand his recruiting area. In the late 1950s, he began to recruit in western Pennsylvania and North Carolina (areas in which he had recruited while he was an assistant at Army). The new areas proved to be very fruitful for the Gophers.

Among his initial recruits were Pennsylvania's Judge Dickson, Bill Munsey and Sandy Stephens, as well as North Carolina's Bobby Bell. Stephens took over as the Gophers quarterback in 1959. The team struggled to a 2–7 record but was competitive, with five of the seven losses being by eight points or less.

Stephens quarterbacked the Gophers to the Rose Bowl following the next two seasons. After the 1961 season, he rushed for 46 yards and two touchdowns and completed 7 of 11 passes for 75 yards to lead the Gophers to a 21–3 victory over UCLA in the Rose Bowl. Following the season, he was named a first-team All-America—the first African American to be named All-America at quarterback for a major college program.

Near Miss

Gophers football coach Bernie Bierman retired following the 1950 season. The first two men to be interviewed for the vacancy were Oklahoma coach Bud Wilkinson and Kentucky coach Bear Bryant (who later gained fame as the Alabama coach), but both men elected to stay in their current positions. Former Ohio State coach Wes Fesler replaced Bierman but stepped down after just three seasons. Fesler was replaced by Murray Warmath.

Cheering On the Gophers

In the fall of 1898, the Gophers took a 3–4 record into a late-season home contest against Northwestern. In an effort to create some interest in the student body, the student newspaper (the *Ariel*) ran an editorial several days before the game, urging students, "any plan that would stir up enthusiasm for athletics would be helpful."

Student Johnny Campbell came up with a plan to lead organized cheers at the game. After the Gophers defeated Northwestern 17–6, Campbell and his "yell leaders" were given credit for the victory and cheerleading was born.

Golden Gophers

In 1857, the year before Minnesota achieved statehood, a newspaper printed a satirical cartoon that pictured nine gophers (with the heads of local politicians) pulling a train. The cartoon was a response to a controversial $5-million railroad proposal in western Minnesota. After the cartoon, Minnesota immediately became known as the "Gopher State."

The University of Minnesota eventually adopted "Gophers" as the nickname for the school's athletic teams. An influential Minneapolis sports writer/radio announcer named Halsey Hall gave an added touch to the school's nickname in the 1930s when, based on the gold jerseys and pants the team wore, he was the first to call them the "Golden Gophers."

TCF Bank Stadium

On September 12, 2009, the Gophers football team played its first game in its new stadium. TCF Bank Stadium, which cost $288.5 million and seats 50,805 (but could eventually be expanded to 80,000 seats) was the first new stadium in the Big Ten Conference since 1960 and the second on-campus stadium built by a major conference school since 1998.

TCF Bank Stadium is the fourth home for the Gophers since 1899. The team played at Northrop Field from 1899 to 1923, Memorial Stadium from 1924 to 1981 and the Metrodome from 1982 to 2008.

Losing Streaks

From October 1974 through to the end of the 1979 season, the Macalester Scots—a small, private St. Paul college team playing an NCAA Division III program—lost an NCAA-record 50 consecutive games. The streak ended when the Scots opened the 1980 season with a 17–14 victory over Mount Senario, a small Wisconsin college.

The University of Minnesota-Morris lost 44 consecutive games—going 0–11 in four consecutive seasons—to set the record for the longest losing streak by an NCAA Division II program. In 2003, after downgrading their program to NCAA Division III, the Cougars lost their first two games to extend the streak to 46 games. They ended the streak on September 20, 2003, with a 61–28 victory over Principia (IL).

Basketball Beginnings

In the fall of 1894, Raymond P. Kaighn enrolled at Hamline University in St. Paul. Kaighn, a protégé of Dr. James Naismith at the Springfield (MA) YMCA, organized Hamline's first basketball team.

Kaighn lined up a game for Hamline against a team from the Minnesota School of Agriculture and Mining (now the St. Paul campus of the University of Minnesota). On February 9, 1895, the Minnesota School defeated Hamline 9–3 in what is considered the first intercollegiate basketball played in the United States.

Two years later, on March 13, 1897, the University of Minnesota played its first game against an outside opponent, defeating a Minneapolis YMCA team 11–5.

Dr. Cooke

Dr. Louis Cooke arrived in Minneapolis in the summer of 1895 to become the director of physical education at the Minneapolis YMCA. In February 1897, he began splitting his duties between the YMCA and the University of Minnesota. Within a year, he was working full time at the University of Minnesota as the basketball coach and director of physical education.

He went on to coach the Gophers for 28 seasons, and his career record of 254–142–3 included three unbeaten seasons (1901–02, 1902–03 and 1918–19). In 1902 and 1919, the Gophers were named the national champions by the Helms Foundation.

Williams Arena

For the first 25 years of the 20th century, the University of Minnesota basketball team played its home games in the University Armory, a small facility used by every athletic team and military drill team on campus.

In 1927, the University began construction on a field house that would become one of the most famous college basketball arenas in the country. On February 4, 1928, with the inventor of basketball—Dr. James Naismith—doing the christening, the University opened its new field house.

The original capacity of the building, which cost $650,000 to build, was 14,100. The building was remodeled in 1950 and renamed Williams Arena in honor of Dr. Henry Williams, the University's first full-time football coach.

From 1950 to 1971, Williams Arena's capacity was 18,025—the largest of any college basketball arena in the country. The arena was remodeled again in 1993, and its capacity was reduced to 14,625.

Williams Arena, with its unique raised floor, is the fifth-oldest Division I college basketball arena in the country. Besides the basketball floor, the arena also contained a hockey rink, which had a seating capacity of about 8000, at the west end of the building. The Gophers hockey team played its final season in the building in 1992–93.

Not the First Choice

Between 1957 and 1970, the University of Minnesota basketball team had just four winning seasons. In that time, the Gophers had just two seasons where they averaged more than 10,000 fans per game.

In April 1971, Minnesota was searching for a new coach for the third time in four seasons. The Gophers were looking for a replacement for George Hanson, who had resigned after one season as the Gophers coach. Hanson had replaced Bill Fitch, who had left after just two seasons to take an NBA coaching job.

The search appeared to be over when Murray State coach Cal Luther agreed to become the Gophers' new coach. But 48 hours after the agreement, he announced he had decided to remain at Murray State. One day later, Minnesota announced that 30-year old Bill Musselman had accepted a four-year contract to coach the Gophers.

For the previous six seasons, Musselman had coached Ashland College—an NCAA Division III program in Ohio—to a 129–30 record. His teams at Ashland were known for two things: defense (two years earlier, Ashland had set a modern NCAA record by allowing just 33.9 points per game) and their program warm-up drills (patterned after the Harlem Globetrotters).

A Controversial Revival

Bill Musselman's first Gopher team quickly caught the attention of Minnesota basketball fans by going

6–3 in the non-conference portion of their schedule. On January 8, 1972, the Gophers opened their Big Ten conference schedule at home against Indiana, which was in its first season under a young coach named Bob Knight.

In front of an overflow crowd of 19,121—the second largest in Williams Arena history—the Gophers pulled out a 52–51 victory over the Hoosiers. The team subsequently defeated Northwestern, Wisconsin and Michigan State to improve to 4–0 in the Big Ten, their best start in conference play in 23 years (they opened the 1948–49 season with a 5–0 record).

Up next for the Gophers was one of the most anticipated games in school history: at home against unbeaten Ohio State. On January 25, 1972, the Buckeyes and the Gophers would play one of the most talked about games in college basketball history.

After the first half, the score was tied 23–23, but the Buckeyes were able to forge a lead in the second half. With less than a minute remaining, the Buckeyes had opened a six-point lead. With 36 seconds remaining, Buckeyes center Luke Witte was fouled and knocked to the floor by Clyde Turner of the Gophers. Turner's foul was ruled flagrant and he was ejected from the game. But before he could leave the floor, a fight started between several players and developed into a bench-clearing brawl.

It took 20 minutes for order to be restored, at which point the game was ruled over. The fight, which sent three Buckeyes to a hospital for treatment, drew immediate national attention and was featured in a two-page spread in the next issue of *Sports Illustrated*.

Three days after the game, Big Ten Commissioner Wayne Duke, who had been in attendance at the game, suspended two Gophers (Corky Taylor and Ron Behagen) for the rest of the season for their roles in the altercation.

But the Gophers regrouped and, with future baseball Hall of Famer Dave Winfield replacing Behagen in the lineup, won seven of their next nine games to win the Big Ten title—the school's first outright conference title since 1919.

From Gophers to Wolves

Bill Musselman coached the Gophers for three more seasons before abruptly resigning in the summer of 1975 to accept a job as the coach of the San Diego team in the ABA. He left town just as an NCAA investigation of the program was getting started. In 1976, the NCAA placed the program on three years of probation for 126 rules infractions, which had occurred during Musselman's stay in Minnesota.

Musselman's stint in San Diego was brief as the team folded just 11 games into the season. But he was able to revive his coaching career and reputation in the minor league Continental Basketball Association (CBA). In five seasons in the CBA, his teams won four league titles.

Shortly after coaching the Albany (NY) Patroons to a 60–10 record and the CBA title, Musselman was named the coach of the expansion Minnesota Timberwolves. He coached the Timberwolves to 22 victories in their first season in league (1989–90) and 29 victories in their second season. He was relieved of his duties after the second season, apparently because of philosophical differences with the team's owners.

After leaving the Timberwolves, Musselman returned to college coaching and coached two seasons at South Alabama. He returned to the NBA as an assistant coach. In 2000, he died from bone marrow cancer at the age of 59.

Vacated Records

Before embarking on a long NBA career, Voshon Lenard was a standout for the University of Minnesota basketball team. During his four-year career with the Gophers (from 1991 to 95), he scored 2103 points in 127 games to become the first player in the program's history to score more than 2000 points.

But according to the NCAA, Lenard scored only 1097 points in 74 games during his Gophers career. There is disagreement over the points total because Lenard's final two seasons with the Gophers (1993–94 and 1994–95) are part of a period in Gophers history that doesn't exist in the eyes of the NCAA.

After an investigation into a scandal in the Gophers basketball program, the school's players were found not to be doing their own academic work. Because of the violations, which the NCAA said occurred over a six-year period, the NCAA ordered the school to vacate all records from six seasons (from 1993 to 1999) and erased Minnesota's name from any postseason appearances during those seasons. So, all records from Lenard's final two seasons with the Gophers (he averaged 18.9 points per game as a junior in 1993–94 and 17.3 points per game as a senior in 1994–95) were vacated.

Clem Haskins, the coach of the Gophers during those years, had his coaching record reduced from 240–165 in 13 seasons to 111–100.

The NCAA erased the Gophers' appearances in the NCAA tournament (in 1994, 1995, 1997 and 1999) and their appearances in the postseason National Invitation Tournament tournament (in 1996 and 1998). The NCAA also vacated the Gophers' appearance in the NCAA Final Four (from 1997) from the record books. The Gophers became the fifth team to have an appearance in the Final Four removed from the records—joining St. Joseph's (1961), Villanova and Western Kentucky (both in 1971) and UCLA (1980).

It Had Happened Before

The expunging of the Gophers' records from 1993 to 1999 wasn't the first time that the NCAA had officially altered Gophers records.

During the 1976–77 season, the Gophers basketball team compiled a 24–3 record. Their only losses were an overtime loss to Purdue and two losses to Michigan.

Early in the season, the talented Gophers—whose starting lineup included three future NBA stars (Kevin McHale, Mychal Thompson and Ray Williams), a future Harlem Globetrotter (Osborne Lockhart) and a future NBA coach (Flip Saunders)—defeated Marquette 66–59 in Milwaukee. Marquette went on to win the NCAA title that season.

But the Gophers, who were on probation for previous NCAA violations, didn't play in the NCAA tournament. After the season, the NCAA ruled that the team had used an ineligible player the entire season and ordered the Gophers to forfeit their 24 victories. In the eyes of the NCAA, the Gophers' 24–3 overall record and 15–3 Big Ten record are 0–27 and 0–18.

Missing Out on a Hall of Fame Coach

In the spring of 1948, the University of Minnesota was looking for a new basketball coach to replace Dave MacMillan, who had resigned after 18 seasons as the Gophers coach.

A young, up-and-coming coach named John Wooden, who had been an All-America at Purdue and had just completed his second season as the coach at Indiana State, was interested in the position. But he was also interested in the coaching vacancy at a California school.

Both schools were interested in Wooden and were supposed to call him on the same day to offer him the job. When Minnesota didn't call—according to newspaper accounts, school officials said phone lines were down because of a snowstorm—and UCLA did, Wooden accepted the UCLA offer.

Over the next 27 seasons, Wooden coached the UCLA Bruins to 10 NCAA titles. During that period, Minnesota employed five different basketball coaches.

Twenty-two years later, the Minnesota athletic program apparently missed a chance at hiring another coaching legend. In 1970, after just two seasons as the Gophers coach, Bill Fitch resigned to accept a job in the NBA.

Bob Knight, who had played at Ohio State and had just finished his fifth season as the coach at Army, was interested in coaching at a Big Ten school. He was reportedly interviewed, but Minnesota elected to promote one of Fitch's assistants, George Hanson, to head coach.

Hanson resigned after just one season as the Gophers coach, so in 1971, Minnesota was looking for its third head coach in four seasons. Knight was still interested in coaching in the Big Ten, but before Minnesota could contact him, he accepted a coaching position at Indiana University.

Late Bloomer

In 1950, George Mikan, who had just led the Minneapolis Lakers to their third consecutive league title, was named the top basketball player for the first 50 years of the 20th century. Although he went on to lead the Lakers to six league titles, he was a late bloomer.

As a 12-year-old, Mikan needed glasses. Two years later, as a freshman at Joliet Catholic High School in Illinois, he was cut from the basketball team because school officials didn't think he could play basketball while wearing glasses.

After graduating from high school, Mikan wanted to play college basketball for Notre Dame, but the coach at the university thought the 6-foot-10 player was too awkward and that his glasses were a hindrance. So, Mikan ended up at DePaul University in Chicago, where a young coach named Ray Meyer developed him into a three-time All-America.

Mikan was inducted into the Basketball Hall of Fame in 1959 and was named one of the NBA's 50 All-time Greatest Players in 2001.

Modest Beginnings

George Keogan, the Notre Dame coach who passed on Mikan, wasn't a coaching novice. Born in Minnesota Lake in 1890 and a graduate of Detroit Lakes High School, he started his coaching career at an Illinois high school in 1910. He became the Notre Dame coach in 1923. Over the next 20 seasons, he coached the Fighting Irish to a 327–96 record. The Fighting Irish, who didn't have a losing season under Keogan, were named the national champions by the Helms Foundation in 1927 and 1928.

On February 15, 1943, Keogan coached the Fighting Irish to a 55–37 victory over Canisius. The victory improved Notre Dame's record to 12–1. Two days later,

Keogan died at the age of 52. He is in the Naismith Memorial Basketball Hall of Fame.

The Pipers

Joe Hutton Sr. was born in Minneapolis and graduated from Excelsior High School before lettering in basketball at Carleton College (in Northfield) for four years.

After college, Hutton embarked on a 40-year coaching career. In 1931, after five seasons as a high school coach, he took over as athletic director and basketball coach at Hamline University in St. Paul.

Over the next 35 seasons, Hutton's Pipers were one of the most recognized and successful small-college basketball programs in the country. Under Hutton, the team won 19 Minnesota Intercollegiate Athletic Conference (MIAC) titles and three national small-college titles.

The Pipers were 591–208 in 35 seasons under Hutton. Among the players Hutton coached were future professional basketball players Vern Mikkelsen and Howie Schultz.

Women's Basketball

In 1891, Canadian Dr. James Naismith was working at the Springfield (MA) YMCA Training School, when he decided an activity was needed for young men in the winter to fill the gap between football in the fall and baseball in the spring.

Naismith's invention—basketball—quickly spread, becoming popular with both men and women. Less than two years after being invented, basketball was being taught to college women in Minnesota.

In 1893, Max Exner, one of Naismith's former roommates, was a student at Carleton College in Northfield, and he introduced the game to the school's female students. By early 1897, just up the road from Northfield, 50 female students at the University of Minnesota formed a women's basketball association. Three years later, the University of Minnesota varsity women's basketball team played its first outside opponent.

Over the next eight seasons, the Minnesota team was one of the top women's basketball teams in the country. During those eight seasons, Minnesota won 46 of 51 games, including 36 of 37 in one five-year stretch.

While the game was very popular with women, as early as 1906, a debate started over intercollegiate athletics for female students. By 1908, the national body that governed amateur athletics outside of high schools and colleges banned women's basketball in public places because they thought it was a bad influence on women—it was considered unfeminine to be seen exercising in public.

The 1907–08 season would be the final intercollegiate season for the Minnesota team.

Women's basketball began disappearing as a sport at the college level before it did at the high school level, and by the early 1920s, basketball—even intramural basketball—for women had stopped in most of the country.

Sport Hangs On in Minnesota

Minnesota was one of just a handful of states where high school girls' basketball survived past the 1920s.

During the 1920s, nearly 200 Minnesota high schools fielded a girls' basketball team. One Minnesota girls' high school basketball team stood out during this era: Grand Meadow won all 94 games it played between 1929 and 1939.

Girls' varsity basketball in the state disappeared after the start of World War II, primarily for financial reasons. Varsity sports for girls didn't reappear in Minnesota high schools until 1969. The first "official" girls' state basketball tournament was held in 1974.

A New Era Begins

Girls' high school basketball, which had disappeared in the state in the early 1940s, reappeared in 1974 when the first "official" state tournament (won by Glencoe) was held. The first star of the new era—from a small rural northern Minnesota town of about 1000 people—would go on to be one of the biggest stars in state history.

Between 1977 and 1979, Janet Karvonen led New York Mills High School to three consecutive state championships. She became the first high school player in state history (boys or girls) to score more than 3000 points in a career (she finished with 3129 points). As a senior, she was named the U.S. High School Player of the Year. She also played collegiately for Old Dominion and Louisiana Tech—appearing in an NCAA Final Four with each of them.

In 2010, Karvonen, who is a member of the National High School Hall of Fame, was in her 22nd year of operating basketball camps for girls.

McCarville and Whalen

During their college careers for the University of Minnesota women's basketball team, Janel McCarville and Lindsay Whalen helped lead the Gophers to their first berth in the NCAA Women's Final Four (in 2004). After making their mark on the Gophers program, they embarked on successful careers in the WNBA.

In the 2004 WNBA draft, Whalen, who had become the program's leading scorer and was a three-time All-America for the Gophers, was the fourth player selected (by the Connecticut Sun). Her selection was the highest a player from the Big Ten Conference had been taken in the WNBA draft.

Whalen's draft distinction would last only a year. McCarville, the only player (male or female) in school history to play in four NCAA tournaments, was the first player taken in the 2005 WNBA draft (by the Charlotte Sting).

In 2010, after six seasons with the Connecticut Sun, Whalen was acquired by the Minnesota Lynx.

Carol Ann Shudlick

During her brilliant four-year career (2000–04) with the Gophers, Lindsay Whalen scored 2285 points to surpass Carol Ann Shudlick (who had scored 2097 points from 1990 to 1994) as the leading scorer in school history.

Shudlick, a two-time All-America for the Gophers, holds the distinction of being the only Gopher to win the Wade Trophy, which is given annually to the top player in women's college basketball. She won the award in 1994.

Shudlick owns the program's single-game scoring record of 44 points (which she did twice). Following her Gophers career, she played professionally in the ABL.

Dick Siebert

Dick Siebert, the son of a Lutheran minister, studied at a seminary before concentrating on a professional baseball career. He made his major league debut in 1932 at the age of 20 and retired following the 1945 season.

In the summer of 1947, he was hired to be the baseball coach at the University of Minnesota. It was the last job he would hold.

Over the next 31 seasons, Siebert coached the Gophers baseball team to 754 victories and three NCAA titles (1956, 1960 and 1964). Future Hall of Famers Paul Molitor and Dave Winfield played for Siebert, making him one of a handful of college baseball coaches who coached two Hall of Famers.

Siebert passed away in December 1978. At the time of his death, he was just one of three college baseball coaches with at least 700 career victories.

Siebert's youngest son, Paul, went on to play in the big leagues.

Jerry Kindall

In the history of NCAA baseball's College World Series (CWS), only one person has both played in and coached a team to an NCAA championship. That person is St. Paul native Jerry Kindall.

In 1956, Kindall hit 18 home runs, drove in 48 runs and batted .381 to lead the University of Minnesota to its first NCAA title. During one of the Gophers' victories at the CWS in Omaha, NE, he hit for the cycle (single, double, triple and home run). That feat hasn't happened at the CWS since.

After the season, Kindall signed with the Chicago Cubs. As an infielder, he went on to play nine seasons in the big leagues (he was with the Twins in 1965) before being released by the Twins in 1966. He became an assistant baseball and basketball coach at the University of Minnesota, and in 1972, he became the head coach at the University of Arizona.

Kindall coached the Wildcats to three NCAA titles before retiring in 1996.

Wrestling Domination

Marcus LeVesseur started his college wrestling career at the University of Minnesota. But after one semester, he transferred to a school less than a mile away—Augsburg College. With the Auggies, LeVesseur would become just one of two wrestlers in the history of college wrestling to go undefeated in his career.

In his first three seasons at Augsburg, LeVesseur, who also played football for the Auggies, went 124–0 and won three NCAA Div. III titles. After taking a year off, he returned for his senior season. He went 31–0 and became the first wrestler in NCAA Div. III history to win four national titles. His career record of 155–0 has been topped only once: Iowa State's Cael Sanderson went 159–0 and won four NCAA Division I wrestling titles in his career (from 1998 to 2002).

Minnesota On Campus Quick Facts

- Frosty Westering, who spent 32 years as the coach of Pacific Lutheran (in Tacoma, WA), spent six seasons (1966–71) at Lea College in Albert Lea before becoming the Lutes coach. Twenty-nine of his 305 career coaching victories (over 40 seasons) came at Lea, which closed in 1973. Westering is a member of the College Football Hall of Fame.
- There are six former University of Minnesota football players in the Pro Football Hall of Fame: Bobby Bell, Carl Eller, Bud Grant, Bronko Nagurski, Leo Nomellini and Charlie Sanders.
- There are 18 former University of Minnesota football players and three former University of Minnesota football coaches in the College Football Hall of Fame. The players are Bronko Nagurski, Bert Baston,

Herb Joesting, Ed Widseth, Dick Wildung, Francis Lund, John McGovern, Ed Rogers, Charles Wilkinson, Bobby Marshall, Bruce Smith, Leo Nomellini, Paul Giel, Clayton Tonnemaker, Bobby Bell, George Franck, Tom Brown and Carl Eller. The coaches are Henry Williams, Fritz Crisler and Bernie Bierman.

- Thirteen University of Minnesota football players were selected in the 1950 NFL draft—Clayton Tonnemaker, Leo Nomellini and Bud Grant were selected in the first round. Also selected were Gordy Soltau, Floyd Jaszewski, Ralph McAllister, Bob Mealey, Gene Fritz, Frank Kuzma, Billy Bye, Ken Beiersdorf, Johnny Lundin and Allen Markert.

Minnesota On Campus Quotables

"The teams that have the best players usually win. It's like a horse race. You can't ride a donkey and win the Kentucky Derby."
–University of Minnesota football coach Murray Warmath

"I've had a lot of fun. Hey, what else is there?"
–former University of Minnesota football player Tom Brown, who played professionally in the CFL and was elected to the College Football Hall of Fame

"When I (visited) Michigan, (coach) Bo Schembechler said it would be a miracle if I played before Dennis Franklin. I appreciated his honesty."
–Michigan native Tony Dungy, who enrolled at the University of Minnesota

Chapter Six

Potpourri

Not in My State!

In the early months of 1891, two Minnesota promoters announced that they would stage a world middleweight championship boxing match in St. Paul during the summer between Australian Bob Fitzsimmons, winner of three world titles, and fellow Australian fighter Jim Hall. Playing host to a boxing match with national appeal was nothing new to Minnesota as some of the greatest fighters of the time had passed through cities like Minneapolis and St. Paul.

But the scheduled match between the two Australians had earned so much national publicity that it aroused the religious reformers in Minnesota who wanted to make boxing illegal. Protests on the streets started soon after the fight was announced, and conservative newspapers published articles denouncing the fight. At first, Governor William R. Merriam refused all demands to halt the fight, but the reformist citizens of St. Paul and Minneapolis continued to grow louder with each passing day and even threatened to impeach him.

The day before the fight, the governor addressed a committee of reformists gathered at the capitol. As reported by the *Minneapolis Tribune*, Merriam told the people gathered, "I doubt, however—and the doubt has been strengthened by consultation with legal gentlemen—that I have the authority to interfere in this matter, except in the case of (a) riot, where it has been shown municipal authorities have not the ability to enforce the law. I will consult with the attorney general on the matter and do what is in my power."

After consulting with his lawyers, Merriam announced that the fight would violate a state statute that banned prizefighting—passed two years earlier but that had been ignored up to that point—and said that the match would be canceled. However, the promoters had a large amount of money on the line and refused to cancel the fight.

On the morning of the fight, the tension in the city was palpable and the governor even considered calling out the National Guard if things got out of control. With pressure mounting and the county sheriff waiting at the arena door to arrest anyone trying to start the match, the organizers decided to cancel the boxing match. Promoter Frank N. Shaw spoke to a *Minneapolis Tribune* reporter after the cancellation, saying, "We have canceled the fight in order to prevent riotous proceedings, as the steps taken by citizens opposing the contest would undoubtedly have led to bloodshed. We are for peace; they are for bloodshed and we want people to understand it."

At the next session of the state legislature, Merriam had a law passed making prizefighting a felony, effectively banning boxing in the entire state of Minnesota. But there was money to be had in boxing, and people just took the scene underground. George Barton, a Minneapolis reporter for over 50 years, wrote in his autobiography published in 1958, "The passage of the anti-prizefighting bill was followed by nearly a quarter-century of illegal 'sneak' fights."

The Return of Boxing

After being illegal in the state for more than 20 years, boxing was legalized in 1915. Minnesota quickly produced several successful boxers, including Johnny Ertle, who won the world bantamweight title in 1915; Mike O'Dowd, who won the world middleweight title in 1917; the Gibbons brothers (Mike and Tommy); Del Flanagan; and Billy Miske.

Tommy Gibbons, who started boxing in 1908, lost only three times in his professional career. His first loss—to Jack Dempsey in 1923—remains one of the most famous fights in boxing history.

In 1923, a group of Shelby, MO, businessmen—including Shelby's mayor—decided to stage a fight in Shelby as a way to promote the area, which was reportedly rich in oil. The group lined up the fight between Gibbons and Dempsey, who had first won the heavyweight title by defeating St. Paul's Billy Miske in 1920.

The fight almost didn't happen. It was canceled once because of financial issues, but at the last minute, the fight was held. On July 4, Dempsey won the fight with a 15-round decision, but it was a financial disaster for the promoters. Only 7700 tickets were sold for the event.

In 1925, Gibbons lost to U.S. light heavyweight champion Gene Tunney by a 12th-round knockout. It was the final fight for Gibbons, who went into a career in law enforcement, serving as the Ramsey County sheriff.

Duane Bobick

Minnesota boxer Duane Bobick, who was born in nearby Little Falls, first gained the national spotlight when he won the gold medal at the 1971 Pan Am Games. The next year, he won the U.S. Golden Gloves heavyweight title and earned a spot on the U.S. Olympic team. At the 1972 Olympics, he reached the gold medal bout, but lost to Cuban Teofilo Stevenson, whom he had beaten a year earlier at the Pan Am Games. The loss ended a 62-match winning streak for Bobick.

After the Olympics, Bobick turned professional. He knocked out his first 19 professional opponents—eventually winning his first 38 professional fights (32 by knockout). One of the victories in that winning streak came in April 1976, when a crowd of 13,789—a record for a bout held in Minnesota—watched him defeat another Minnesota heavyweight, Scott LeDoux. Also in 1976, Bobick reportedly had a contract agreement to fight Muhammad Ali, but the fight never happened.

Bobick's winning streak came to end in a loss to Ken Norton in May 1977. Ranked as high as No. 5 in the heavyweight rankings, he retired in 1979 at the age of 28. He was 48–4 as a professional.

Bobick's younger brother, Rodney, was also a professional boxer. Rodney Bobick, who turned pro in March 1972, won his first 10—and 32 of his first 35—professional fights. Rodney died in a car crash in June 1977. At 26, he had a 37–7 record (with 18 knockouts) as a pro.

Moonlighting

George Barton's newspaper career lasted 55 years. When not working as a journalist, he had a part-time job—as a boxing referee.

In the first half of the 20th century, he refereed nearly every major bout in the Upper Midwest. In all, he worked more than 12,000 fights, including bouts of boxing legends Jack Dempsey and Gene Tunney.

Ring Magazine ranks Barton as one of the top five boxing officials of all time.

Wrestling Legends

Long before Brock Lesnar left the University of Minnesota and achieved fame in professional wrestling and as a mixed martial arts fighter, several other former University of Minnesota athletes became legends of the wrestling ring.

The first was Bronko Nagurski, who is a member of the College Football Hall of Fame and the Pro Football Hall of Fame. Nagurski began his professional wrestling career during the football off-season (while playing for the Chicago Bears of the NFL). During his wrestling career, he won the world heavyweight wrestling title three times—1937, 1939 and 1941.

Another former Gopher who fared well in football and wrestling was Leo Nomellini. He earned All-America honors for the Gophers football team in 1949 before enjoying a long, successful NFL career, and he also moonlighted in wrestling during the football off-seasons. In 1956, Nomellini and Verne Gagne teamed up to win the World Tag Team title. Like Nagurski, Nomellini is a member of the College Football and NFL Halls of Fame.

Bud Smith wrestled and played football for the University of Minnesota before serving in the U.S. Navy during World War II. Following his military service, he changed his name to Stan "Krusher" Kowalski and turned to professional wrestling. In a 25-year career—from 1951 to 1976—he wrestled more than 6000 matches and won 19 titles. Kowalski and his tag-team partner—Tiny Mills—were known as "Murder Inc."

Verne Gagne

Verne Gagne entered the University of Minnesota in the fall of 1943 and won his first Big Ten Conference in wrestling as a freshman. After a two-year stint in the military, he resumed his Gophers career in 1946, winning Big Ten titles in 1947, 1948 and 1949 and NCAA titles in 1948 and 1949.

After college, Gagne briefly considered a pro football career (he was drafted by the Chicago Bears and spent time in the Green Bay Packers training camp) before deciding to focus on wrestling in 1949. For the next 36 years, he was the face of professional wrestling in the Upper Midwest.

In 1960, he formed the American Wrestling Association (AWA), and the organization would dominate wrestling in the Upper Midwest for much of the second half of the 20th century. The AWA's weekly television show was a must-see for Minnesota wrestling fans. Gagne won the AWA's heavyweight 10 times.

A Legend on the Links

Before she became interested in golf, women's golf legend Patty Berg was interested in another sport. While growing up in south Minneapolis, she played on a neighborhood youth football team called the 50th Street Tigers. One of her teammates was Bud Wilkinson, who would go on to make a name for himself in college football.

Berg finally took up golf at the age of 13 and played in her first amateur tournament at 16. After being named the *Associated Press* Female Athlete of the Year in 1938, she won 28 tournaments as an amateur and turned professional in June 1940.

Berg's professional golf career was interrupted by World War II when, in 1942, she enlisted in the marines. She eventually became a lieutenant. During her three years in the marines, while on leave from her military duty, she won her first two professional tournaments (even though she was rarely able to practice).

In 1943, she was named the Female Athlete of the Year for the second time.

In 1946, Berg won the first U.S. Women's Open. Four years later, she was one of the founders of the Ladies Professional Golf Association (LPGA) and served as the organization's first president.

She went on to win 44 tournaments between 1948 and 1962.

A Golfing Mentor

If John Mariucci is the godfather of Minnesota hockey, Les Bolstad is the godfather of Minnesota golf.

In 1926, at the age of 18, Bolstad became the youngest golfer to win the U.S. Amateur Public Links Championship. The next year, as a student at the University of Minnesota, he won medalist honors at the Big Ten Conference meet. In 1929, he won his second Big Ten Conference title.

From 1946 to 1976, Bolstad coached the golf team at the University of Minnesota. In addition to coaching the Gophers, he also mentored many of the state's golfers, including Patty Berg.

Persistence Pays Off

After growing up in Alexandria, Tom Lehman enrolled at the University of Minnesota. He earned All-America honors three times (1979, 1980 and 1981)—the only golfer in school history to do so—before he turned professional.

But success as a professional golfer didn't come easily. After limited success on the PGA tour from

1983 to 1985 (his top finish was a tie for 11th place and he earned just $39,000 in his first three seasons) Lehman spent the next six years on golf's minor professional tours.

His first professional victory came on the Ben Hogan Tour (now called the Nationwide Tour) in 1990. He won three more tournaments on the Hogan Tour before rejoining the PGA Tour full-time in 1992.

His first PGA Tournament victory came in May 1994 at the Memorial. In 1996, he won the British Open and was named the PGA's Player of the Year.

In 2009, Lehman began splitting his time between the PGA Tour and the PGA Champions Tour (players can begin playing at the age of 50). In April 2009, a little over a month past his 50th birthday, he became the first Champions Tour player to win his tour debut when he teamed with Bernhard Langer to win the Liberty Mutual Legends of Golf.

On May 30, 2010, Lehman earned his second Champions Tour victory with a victory at the Senior PGA Championship. Through the 2010 season, he ranked No. 25 on the PGA's career money list, having earned $21.25 million.

Hilary Lunke

Hilary Homeyer Lunke of Edina picked one of the LPGA tour's major championships at which to win her first professional tournament, and she worked overtime to do it.

In 2003, in Portland, OR, Lunke defeated Angela Stanford and Kelly Robbins in an 18-hole playoff to win the U.S. Women's Open. She was the first player in United States Golf Association (USGA) history to win the U.S. Open after advancing through local and section qualifying. Her first-place prize money was $560,000—the largest winner's share in LPGA history up to that point.

Through the 2010 LPGA season, it was the only victory of Lunke's LPGA career. She was elected president of the LPGA Player Executive Committee in 2008.

Surviving the Cuts

In April 2002, the University of Minnesota announced that it was dropping its men's golf program effective in 2003 in a cost-cutting move. Three weeks after the announcement, the Gophers men's golf team won the Big Ten Conference championship—the school's first conference title in 30 years.

About a month after the Big Ten meet, the Gophers surprised many observers by winning their first-ever NCAA title. It wasn't easy. The tournament, which was held at Ohio State's Scarlet Course in Columbus, OH, was hampered by rain the first two days and more rain was forecasted for the third day.

NCAA officials discussed cutting the tournament's 30-team field in half for the final two rounds, and had the NCAA made that move, the Gophers wouldn't have had the opportunity to win the tournament. After the first two rounds, the team was in 16th place, one stroke out of 15th place—the cutoff if the NCAA trimmed the field. But the NCAA decided to let all 30 teams finish the tournament.

Despite more rain and heavy winds in the third round, the Gophers moved up 12 spots to fourth place, heading into the tournament's final day.

On the final day, the Gophers shot a 6-under par, 278 to finish with a 72-hole total of 1134 and become the first "northern" school to win the NCAA title since 1979. They were the only team in the field to shoot under par in each of the last two rounds, and they edged pre-tournament favorite Georgia Tech by four strokes.

The Gophers were led by Justin Smith, who shot a final-round 69 to finish in a tie for fourth place with a 279—three strokes behind medalist Troy Matteson of Georgia Tech. Smith was the only player in the field who didn't have a round over par.

The team's previous best at the NCAA meet was a second-place finish in 1944. In the 58 years between, their best finish was seventh place in 1998.

School administrators gave the program a deadline of February 1, 2003, to raise $1.8 million for the program to survive past the 2003 season. Two months after the announcement, supporters of the program had already raised $900,000. The goal was reached and the program survived.

The U.S. Amateur

The United States Golf Association (USGA) conducted its first U.S. Amateur Championship in 1901. In the 109 years since, only two native Minnesotans have won the tournament.

In 1929, at Pebble Beach, CA, St. Paul's Harrison "Jimmy" Johnston won the tournament. It would be more than 50 years before another Minnesotan claimed the victory.

In 1993, Roseau native John Harris won the tournament in Houston, TX. Harris, who had played hockey and golf at the University of Minnesota, defeated Danny Ellis of Haines City, FL, in the finals of match play. Two years earlier, in Chattanooga, TN, Harris was the co-leader after two rounds of stroke play at the U.S. Amateur but lost in the first round of match play.

Getting Started

In June 1893, the Town and Country Club in St. Paul was losing members. It had sought to boost support by adding summer pastimes such as lawn tennis and croquet, but club membership continued to dwindle.

The club got the attention of Scottish golf enthusiast George W. McRee and went to work mowing out the first golf green west of New Jersey. It wasn't the most sophisticated of courses at first with tomato cans as cups and fishing poles for flags, but the sport eventually caught on with members and the course improved and expanded. The club and course remain to this day.

The World's Game

Major league professional soccer had a relatively brief, albeit memorable, stay in Minnesota.

One month into their first North American Soccer League (NASL) season, the Minnesota Kicks drew the largest crowd in NASL history. A little over five years later, the Kicks were gone.

The team arrived in Minnesota in 1976 after spending the previous two seasons in Denver. Their first home match in Minnesota, on May 9, 1976, had to be delayed for 15 minutes because so many people were waiting to buy tickets. The game started after about 2000 fans were let in free.

One month later, on June 9, an NASL-record crowd of 46,164 showed up at Metropolitan Stadium to watch the New York Cosmos and Pelé, the greatest player in the history of the sport, defeat the Kicks 2–1.

Following their inaugural season, the Kicks set an NASL-playoff attendance record twice in a five-day span. A 3–0 victory over Seattle was played in front of 41,505 fans. Four days later, a sellout crowd of 49,571 saw the team defeat San Jose 3–1 and advance to the NASL Championship game, where they lost 3–1 to Toronto.

The Kicks won a division title in each of their first four seasons and reached the playoffs in each of their six seasons in Minnesota. They were second or third in league attendance in each of their first four seasons (averaging 23,117 per game in 1976; 32,771 in 1977; 30,860 in 1978 and 24,580 in 1979).

In the fall of 1981, the team was in a dispute over a new lease (Metropolitan Stadium was in its final year of use) with the Metrodome for the 1982 season. Kicks owner Ralph Sweet, who had owned the franchise less than a year, threatened to relocate the franchise because it was losing money. The league office stepped in and folded the franchise after Sweet withheld players' payroll checks.

Trio of Stars

In their six seasons in Minnesota, the Kicks featured three of the top five scorers in NASL history.

Alan Willey is third in league history with 306 points (129 goals and 48 assists). Ron Futcher is fourth with 296 points (119 goals and 58 assists) and Ace Ntsoelengoe is fifth with 256 points (87 goals and 82 assists).

Only one player in league history, Giorgio Chinaglia, scored more goals (193) than Willey.

Another Chance

Following the demise of the Minnesota Kicks, the state was without professional soccer for only two years.

In 1984, the Fort Lauderdale Strikers relocated to Minnesota. The wife of Joe Robbie, a Minneapolis lawyer who owned the Miami Dolphins of the NFL, owned the team, and their first season in Minnesota was highlighted by the largest crowd to see a soccer match in state history.

On May 28, 1984, in the team's fifth game of the season, a Metrodome crowd of 52,621 watched the Strikers defeat the Tampa Bay Rowdies 1–0. Many of the fans stayed after the match to watch a free concert put on by the Beach Boys.

Following their inaugural season, the team was one of four NASL teams that joined the Major Indoor Soccer

League (MISL). In their second season in the MISL, they advanced to the finals of the league's playoffs.

Facing the San Diego Sockers, the Strikers took a 3–1 lead in their best-of-seven series to move within one victory of becoming the first Minnesota professional team to win a league title in 32 years. The Sockers rallied to win the series 4–3 and earn their fifth consecutive MISL championship.

Just two years later, the Strikers folded because of financial difficulties.

Overcoming Obstacles

St. Paul native Tommy Milton began driving race cars on county fair dirt tracks around Minnesota in 1913. Ten years later, he was the most famous racer in America.

In 1917, Milton defeated several well-known racers in a 100-mile race. In 1920, he set a record speed of 155 mph, which would stand for six years.

Milton gained national attention in 1921 when he won the Indy 500. He was one of only eight drivers (out of a starting field of 20 drivers) to finish the 1921 Indy 500, winning the race with an average speed of 81.62 mph.

Two years later, Milton enhanced his reputation when he became the first driver to win the Indy 500 twice, averaging 91.4 mph to win the 1923 Indy 500. He was just one of 11 drivers (out of 24) to finish the race, despite suffering severely blistered hands incurred during the race, requiring treatment at a hospital.

Milton retired from racing in 1931. He had 23 victories in his racing career and, at the time of his retirement, held 50 records.

In 1958, he was part of the inaugural class inducted into the Minnesota Sports Hall of Fame. The *Minneapolis Tribune* pointed out that Milton had achieved success in racing despite being "so blind in one eye, he couldn't pass the road test."

The Professor of Pro Stock

Virginia native Warren Johnson competed in a National Hot Rod Association (NHRA) event for the first time in 1971, and he was still competing on the NHRA circuit 39 years later.

In May 2010, at the age of 66, Johnson won the Pro Stock event at the Midwest Nationals in Madison, IL, to become the oldest driver to win a race in NHRA history. That victory was the 97th of his professional career.

Johnson, who in 1997 became the first NHRA Pro Stock Driver to surpass 200 mph, was elected to the International Motorsports Hall of Fame in 2007.

Minnesota Sports Quick Facts

- In the early 1900s, at least two Minnesotans gained national prominence in wrestling: St. Paul's Walter Miller won three world titles between 1914 and 1924, and Norwegian immigrant Henry Ordemann of Minneapolis held the American heavyweight title from 1910 to 1914.
- After competing at Minneapolis Roosevelt High School and the University of Minnesota, Fortune Gordien

was a three-time U.S. Olympian. Gordien held the world record in the discus throw for nine years.

Minnesota Sports Quotables

"Wrestling is ballet with violence."
—former Minnesota governor and pro wrestler Jesse Ventura

"I ain't got time to bleed."
—Jesse Ventura

"My governor can beat up your governor."
—popular t-shirt after the election of Jesse Ventura

Chapter Seven

Stadium Debates

The First Stadium Debate

Minnesota is known as the "Land of 10,000 Lakes." In truth, the motto displays modesty—Minnesota actually has 11,482 lakes of 10 acres or more.

Looking over the last 50 years, it seems Minnesota's motto should be "Land of 10,000 Stadium Debates." Actually, the first stadium controversy in Minnesota was more than 120 years ago.

Professional baseball came to Minneapolis for good with the Minneapolis Millers in 1884 (the first attempt, in 1877, lasted only one season). Just five years later, the first stadium debate developed. In early 1889, the Minneapolis City Council decided to build a downtown ballpark for the Millers. The decision was greeted by much dissension, especially from those who were concerned with baseball being played in the city on a Sunday. The plan for a ballpark went ahead and the new field, called Athletic Park, opened on May 16, 1889.

It didn't take long for the next stadium controversy to appear. In May 1896, the Millers were given a 30-day eviction notice because the site of the ballpark was going to be redeveloped for other use. The Millers played their final game at Athletic Park on May 23, 1896, and embarked on a long road trip, not knowing where they would play when they returned to Minneapolis.

The city quickly considered four sites before choosing a location just south of downtown for the new ballpark. The new field, which eventually would be called Nicollet Park, was built in three weeks and the Millers played their first game there on June 19. The ballpark, which cost $4000 to build, was the Millers' home for the next 59 years.

Debates Take On New Meaning

By the early 1950s, the ballpark debates took on new meaning as civic and business leaders in Minneapolis and St. Paul thought a new stadium would lure either a major league baseball team or a pro football franchise to the area.

On November 3, 1953, voters in St. Paul passed a city bond issue (by a 71.6 percent to 28.3 percent margin), which included $2 million to build Midway Stadium, which the city said could house a major league team.

Less than a year later, a commission backed by the cities of Bloomington, Minneapolis and Richfield purchased a 164-acre site for $478,899 in Bloomington.

Metropolitan Stadium, the future home of the Minnesota Twins and the Minnesota Vikings, was built on the site. The stadium opened in 1956, and its first tenant was the Minneapolis Millers, who played their final five seasons there.

A Short Break from Debates

When Metropolitan Stadium opened in 1956, some baseball observers described it as "the last word in stadium construction." Its cantilever construction meant there were no obstructed-view seats. Still, Metropolitan Stadium provided only a short break from the stadium debates.

The Minnesota Twins and the Minnesota Vikings began play in the stadium in 1961. Just eight years later, talk of the need to replace the 48,000-seat stadium—its final price tag, which included renovations in the 1960s, was $10.3 million—surfaced.

In 1975, Governor Wendell Anderson urged replacing Metropolitan Stadium or risk losing the Twins and the Vikings. After three years of political debate, the Minnesota Legislature finally passed a stadium bill in 1977.

But the debate lingered over the cost and site of a new stadium. Eight proposals were considered before a location was finally chosen on the east end of downtown Minneapolis.

Construction of the Hubert H. Humphrey Metrodome began on December 20, 1979. The multipurpose stadium, with a price tag of $55 million, was completed in 28 months—on schedule and under budget.

Fittingly, when the Minnesota Twins played their first regular-season game in their new home on April 6, 1982, it was 28 degrees outside.

Stadium Debates Not Over

The opening of the Metrodome only temporarily ended the stadium debates in Minnesota.

By the late 1990s, the Minnesota Twins, who had eight consecutive losing seasons between 1993 and 2000, expressed a need for their own stadium; the Metrodome was considered a better stadium for football than it was for baseball.

In January 1997, Governor Arne Carlson and Twins owner Carl Pohlad announced an agreement in which the Twins would contribute $90 million toward a $350 million stadium. As part of the deal, the state would get a minority interest in the team.

Before the end of the year, the deal had fallen through. In October 1997, Pohlad announced he had a tentative agreement to sell the Twins to a North Carolina businessman named Don Beaver for $150 million. A month later, the Minnesota House of Representatives voted 84–47 against a new stadium.

The deal with Beaver had a deadline of March 31, 1998. The deadline passed and in May 1998, voters in Greensboro, NC, voted down a bill to build a baseball stadium.

In March 1999, voters in St. Paul voted down a 0.5 percent sales tax increase to pay for a baseball stadium in St. Paul. If the referendum had passed, Pohlad was going to sell the Twins to Glen Taylor, who owned the Timberwolves, and Robert Naegele, the principal owner of the Minnesota Wild.

In 2001, the debate about the Twins' future got louder after they were reportedly targeted for contraction by the MLB. In 2006, after threats of moving by the Twins and political debate filled with rancor, the Minnesota Legislature passed a bill for a new stadium for the Twins.

The Twins moved into their new $588 million stadium, Target Field, in 2010.

Debate Over New Football Stadium

The Minnesota Vikings, whose lease at the Metrodome expires after the 2011 season, say they need a new stadium. The Vikings, whose stadium revenue is among the lowest in the NFL, say they can't compete financially if they remain in the Metrodome.

In 2010, the Vikings were the sole full-time tenants of the Metrodome. The University of Minnesota football team, which played in the Metrodome from 1982 to 2008, began play in its new on-campus stadium in 2009.

Minnesota Stadium Quick Facts

- The Metrodome is the only stadium in the U.S. to play host to a World Series, an MLB All-Star game, the Super Bowl and the NCAA men's basketball Final Four. In 1987, the first World Series game to be played indoors was played at the Metrodome.

- The former site of Metropolitan Stadium in Bloomington is now occupied by the Mall of America. A plaque in the mall denotes where Metropolitan Stadium's home plate had been.

Minnesota Stadium Quotables

"It (Metropolitan Stadium) was a hell of a business venture. The people built it with private money. There was no bond issue, no government or city money. They were very happy with it and had a different feeling about the park. It was their park."

–Twins owner Calvin Griffith

"You know there are always people who say 'you won't see me going to a game in a dome.' It's like when the Met (Metropolitan Stadium) was built, St. Paul people said they wouldn't go to Bloomington. But you always end up seeing them at games. I think once you get baseball in your blood, you'll go to the games no matter where they're played."

–Twins owner Calvin Griffith

"This is the first time in at least eight years we've got a governor who says, 'I want to do it.'"

–Metropolitan Sports Facilities Chairman Ted Mondale, speaking of newly elected Governor Mark Dayton and a bill for a new Vikings stadium

"Our focus is entirely on making sure they're successful here in this market."

–NFL Commissioner Roger Goodell, regarding the Vikings and their potential move if a new stadium isn't built

Chapter Eight

Let's Not Forget

Dan Patch

The most well-known horse in the United States over the first 20 years of the 20th century was a Minnesotan pacer named Dan Patch.

Dan Patch started racing in 1900 at the age of 4. Between 1900 and 1902, when he stopped racing against other pacers, he was unbeaten. After being purchased in 1902 by a Minnesota businessman named Marion W. Savage for $60,000—$1.54 million in 2009 dollars—Patch raced only against the clock.

Before being retired in 1909, Patch set 10 world records and made Savage an estimated $2 million ($48.6 million in 2009). The horse, which was transported around the country in a private railroad car, was so valuable to Savage that he reportedly had it insured for $50,000.

Patch died on July 11, 1916, at the age of 20. At the time of the horse's death, Savage was in a Minneapolis hospital recovering from minor surgery. The next day, about 30 hours after Patch's death, Savage suffered a heart attack and died at the age of 57.

A Brief Layover

Amelia Earhart gained fame as the first female pilot to fly the Atlantic Ocean solo. But 15 years before making her mark as an aviator, Earhart was like many other high school girls in Minnesota: interested in basketball.

Earhart spent her junior year of high school (in 1913–14) at St. Paul Central High School. She spent only one year in St. Paul before her family moved to Chicago. After graduating from a Chicago high school, she attended Ogontz School (a finishing school for girls in Pennsylvania) where she played basketball.

She later coached several girls' basketball teams before beginning her aviation career. She took her first flying lesson in 1921. In June 1928, Earhart made her famous trans-Atlantic flight.

A Novel Idea

In 1922, 18-year-old Ralph Samuelson of Lake City (on the Mississippi River) set out to prove that if it was possible to ski on snow, it should be possible to ski on water.

He purchased 15-pound, 9-foot-long pine boards from a lumberyard and boiled and curled the tips. He strapped them on his feet and hitched himself to a motorboat. Within several days, he was waterskiing on nearby Lake Pepin.

As an adult, in his spare time from his job as a turkey farmer, Samuelson put on shows and demonstrations around the country. It wasn't until 1967 that the American Water Ski Association certified him as the inventor of waterskiing.

Making a Splash

Besides basketball, there was a second sport popular with Minnesota high school girls in the 1920s and 1930s: swimming. Between 1924 and 1942, a girls' state high school swimming meet was held yearly in Minnesota.

The first standout in the sport was Ann Govednik of Chisholm. From 1931 to 1934, she dominated two events at the state meet, winning four state titles in the 50-yard breaststroke and four state titles in the 100-yard breaststroke.

Three weeks after the 1932 state meet, where she had set new state records in two events, Govednik set a world record in the 100-yard breaststroke. Under AAU auspices, in Virginia, she swam the event in 1:18.9. Less than two weeks after turning 16, she swam in the 1932 Summer Olympics, finishing sixth in the 200-meter breaststroke.

Govednik ended her high school career at the 1934 state meet by winning the two events again. She went on to compete in the 1936 Olympics.

Art Johlfs

Minneapolis real estate agent Art Johlfs was a pioneer. More than 50 years before *USA Today* began offering national rankings in high school sports like basketball and football, he was the first to compile national high school rankings.

In 1927, Johlfs, a former basketball coach, began national high school football rankings. He continued his rankings through his *National Sports News Service* newsletter for more than 50 years. He added boys' basketball rankings in 1944 and girls' basketball rankings in 1975.

When he retired in 1978, he turned his rankings over to an Arizona high school sports historian named Barry Sollenberger. In 1999, *Student Sports* took over the rankings.

A Really Big Show

Nick Kahler, who gained fame as a hockey player with the St. Paul Athletic Club and as the founder of the Minneapolis Millers minor league hockey team, made another lasting contribution to Minnesota.

In 1933, he founded the Northwest Sports Show. The show, held annually in March, is the longest-running sports show in the United States. The show was so popular in the 1950s that it had scheduling priority at the Minneapolis Auditorium over the NBA-champion Minneapolis Lakers.

Ice Follies

One of the most popular figure skating shows in U.S. history was founded by a St. Paul chemist and a typewriter salesman.

Oscar Johnson and Eddie Shipstad began performing a comedy doubles skating routine at the Hippodrome Figure Skating Club in St. Paul in the early 1920s. They eventually performed the act between periods at minor league hockey games in the Upper Midwest and in Boston and Chicago.

In October 1936, the Shipstad and Johnson Ice Follies performed at the Minneapolis Auditorium for the first time. One month later, the show went on tour—with 36 skaters—for the first time.

Lindsey Vonn

Minnesota native Lindsey Vonn is the most successful American female in ski racing history. Vonn, who turned in 26 in 2010, began skiing at the age of two before joining a development program at Buck Hill (in Burnsville). She won three consecutive World Cup and downhill titles from 2008–10, the first American woman (and the second woman in the world) to accomplish this. She won the gold medal in downhill at the 2010 Winter Olympics.

Before Hollywood

In 1943 and 1944, an athlete from Minneapolis Southwest High School named Peter Aurness took first place in the 120-yard high hurdles at the Minnesota State High School Track Meet.

Following his high school graduation, Aurness spent two years in the Army Air Forces before returning to Minnesota to study drama at the University of Minnesota. He eventually followed in the footsteps of his older brother James, who had moved to Los Angeles to pursue an acting career.

When James Aurness signed his first movie contract, the studio changed the spelling of his last name to Arness. He went on to a long television career as the star of "Gunsmoke."

When Peter Aurness signed his first movie contract, he took the last name Graves. Graves went on to a long, successful career in movies and television. His most famous role was in the television series "Mission: Impossible."

Graves passed away in March 2010, four days shy of his 84th birthday.

Embracing Winter

Winter is hard to escape in the Upper Midwest. So, rather than fight it, some Minnesotans have given into it.

The city of St. Paul has celebrated winter with its Winter Carnival since 1888.

From 1966 to 1982, the Carnival was kicked off by a snowmobile race called the International 500. The race, which was from Winnipeg, MB to St. Paul, MN, was the longest snowmobile race in the world. Needless to say, it was only for the hardiest of snowmobile drivers.

In 1969, only 19 of the 118 snowmobilers who started the race finished it. In 1972, it was –37 degrees at the race's start and only about half the field (162 of 301) finished the first leg (176 miles).

Upon Further Review

For nearly 50 years, Admiral Robert E. Peary was given credit for being the first person to reach the North Pole. But in 1988, 79 years after he reportedly had reached the pole, the National Geographic Society said that a review of Peary's diary showed he had actually missed the pole by at least 30 miles.

The first person to reach the North Pole is now considered to be Ralph Plaisted of St. Paul. In 1967, his first attempt fell short. But in April 1968, after 43 days and 474 miles by snowmobile, his group reached the pole.

In 1990, Ely's Will Steger, who had reached the North Pole in 1986, became the first person to travel Antarctica at its widest distance.

In 1993, Minnesotan Ann Bancroft, who three years earlier had become the first woman to reach the North Pole (as part of Steger's expedition), became the first woman to reach both poles when she reached the South Pole by ski.

In 2001, Bancroft and Liv Arenson became the first women to ski across Antarctica.

The Natural

Cindy Nelson grew up around skiing, and her family owned a ski resort along Minnesota's North Shore.

She made her first U.S. national skiing team as a 15-year-old. In 1974, she became the first American to win a World Cup downhill race. Two years later, at the 1976 Innsbruck Olympics, she won a bronze medal in the downhill event.

Before her retirement from international skiing in 1985, she won seven World Cup races and seven U.S. National championships.

During her career, Nelson, who spent 14 years as a member of the national team, became the first woman to be a member of four U.S. National teams.

Minnesota Sports Facts

• At the 2002 Winter Olympics in Salt Lake City, 21 Minnesota-born athletes—more than any other state—represented the United States. At the 2006 Winter Games, 34 Minnesotans proudly represented their country. Hennepin and Ramsey Counties have produced 108 Winter Olympians as of 2006.

• Born in St. Paul in 1921, artist LeRoy Neiman was the official artist for five Olympic Games (Summer 1972, Winter 1976, Winter 1980, Winter and Summer 1984).

• Minneapolis native John Johnson was a champion cyclist and speed skater. In 1892, at 19 years of age, he became the first person to cycle one mile in less than two minutes when he went 1:56.6. He also was a fast speed skater, setting several records in his day. He is a member of the Minnesota Sports Hall of Fame.

• Born in St. Paul, Dorothy Franey Langkop was one of the best female speed skaters of her day. She won three U.S. and North American championships and a bronze medal in the 1000 meters at the 1932 Olympics. At one time, she held five U.S. speed skating records. For all her accomplishments, she was added to the Minnesota Sports Hall of Fame.

• Amy Peterson was a champion speed skater and Winter Olympian. The Maplewood native won three individual medals in five Olympic appearances, including a silver medal in 1992 and two bronze in 1994.

• In 2006, at the Turin Winter Olympics in Italy, the Pete Fenson Rink (from Bemidji) won the bronze medal in curling. Team member Scott Baird became the oldest American to earn a medal at the Winter Olympics: he was three months shy of his 55th birthday.

• Tom Malchow became the first Minnesota native to win a gold medal in an individual event in the Summer Olympics when he won a gold medal at the 2000 Games in Sydney. The 6-foot-6 Malchow, who was a silver medalist at the Atlanta Games in 1996, won the gold in the 200-meter butterfly.

• St. Paul's Jeanne Arth was the first Minnesotan to play at Wimbledon. In 1959, Arth and Californian Darlene Hard teamed to win the doubles championship at Wimbledon. Arth and Hard had also won the doubles title at the U.S. Championships in 1958 and 1959.

- Former Governor Jesse Ventura's real name is actually James George Janos, and he was inducted into the World Wrestling Entertainment Hall of Fame in 2004. Before becoming governor, he was once a bodyguard for The Rolling Stones.

Minnesota Sports Quotables

"Adventure is worthwhile in itself."

–Amelia Earhart

"Women, like men, should try to do the impossible. And when they fail, their failure should be a challenge to others."

–Amelia Earhart

"I have a pretty good support team with my husband, my agent, the U.S. Ski Team and all of my personal sponsors."

–Lindsey Vonn

"I feel really fortunate to be in a position now to be a positive role model for younger kids. I think they need more of that these days."

–Lindsey Vonn

"The 2010 Olympic season was incredible, but what made it so special is that I was able to share it with so many American fans. It was amazing to see the support and excitement they showed for ski racing and that's definitely carried into this winter. It means so much to the athletes to hear from them. Win or crash, they keep us excited to compete."

–Lindsey Vonn

Chapter Nine

Minnesota Hall of Fame

Auto Racing
- Tommy Milton (1958)

Baseball
- Charles Albert Bender (1958)
- Rod Carew (2006)
- Calvin Griffith (1986)
- Mike Kelley (1959)
- Tom Kelly (2006)
- Harmon Killebrew (1972)
- Tony Oliva (1988)
- Kirby Puckett (2006)
- Dick Siebert (1987)
- Dave Winfield (2006)

Basketball
- Dr. L.J. Cooke (1963)
- Lou Hudson (2006)
- Joe Hutton Sr. (1972)
- Janet Karvonen (1989)
- John Kundla (1990)

- George Mikan (1958)
- Vern Mikkelsen (1988)

Bicycling

- John Johnson (1959)

Bowling

- Jean Havlish (1988)

Boxing

- Tommy Gibbons (1958)
- Mike Gibbons (1958)
- Mike O'Dowd (1958)

Curling

- Bob Dunbar (1958)

Figure Skating

- Robin Lee (1963)

Football

- Bobby Bell (2006)
- Bernie Bierman (1958)
- Gil Dobie (1963)
- Carl Eller (1989)
- Paul Giel (1990)
- Bud Grant (1987)
- William W. Heffelfinger (1958)
- Pug Lund (1990)
- Bobby Marshall (1988)
- Jim Marshall (1986)
- Earl Martineau (1972)
- John McGovern (1958)

- Clarence Munn (1963)
- Bronko Nagurski (1958)
- Alan Page (1989)
- Bruce Smith (1986)
- Sandy Stephens (2006)
- Fran Tarkenton (1987)
- Murray Warmath (2006)
- Edwin Widseth (1963)
- Charles Wilkinson (1972)
- Dr. Henry L. Williams (1958)
- Max Winter (1987)

Golf

- Patty Berg (1958)
- Les Bolstad (1972)
- Harrison Johnston (1958)

Handball

- George Quam (1963)

Hockey

- Frank Brimsek (1988)
- Herb Brooks (1990)
- Walter Bush (1989)
- Frank Goheen (1958)
- Nick Kahler (1963)
- John Mariucci (1986)
- John Mayasich (1987)

Horse Racing

- George Loomis (1963)

Media
- Halsey Hall (1989)
- Jimmy Robinson (1972)

Rifle
- Emmett Swanson (1959)

Rowing
- Walter Hoover (1985)

Skiing
- Cindy Nelson (1990)

Speedboat Racing
- Garfield Wood (1959)

Speed Skating
- Ken Bartholomew (1959)
- Dorothy Langkop (1963)

Tennis
- Jeanne Arth (1986)

Track and Field
- Fortune Gordien (1958)

Women's Athletics Pioneer
- Dorothy McIntyre (2006)

Wrestling
- Verne Gagne (2006)

Notes on Sources

Book Sources

Barton, George. *My Lifetime in Sports.* Minneapolis: Olympic Press, 1958.

Brackin, Dennis and Patrick Reusse. *Minnesota Twins: The Complete Illustrated History.* Minneapolis: MVP Books, an imprint of MBI Publishing and the Quayside Publishing Group, 2010.

Gillete, Gary, ed. *The ESPN Pro Football Encyclopedia,* first edition. New York: Sterling Publishing, 2006.

Hartman, Sid with Joel Rippel. *Sid Hartman's Great Minnesota Sports Moments.* St. Paul, Minn.: Voyageur Press, an imprint of MBI Publishing, 2006.

Hugunin, Marc and Stew Thornley. *Minnesota Hoops: Basketball in the North Star State.* St. Paul, Minn.: Minnesota Historical Society Press, 2006.

Johnson, Lloyd and Miles Wolff, ed. *Encyclopedia of Minor League Baseball, third edition.* Durham, N.C.: Baseball America, Inc., 2007.

Johnson, Lloyd, ed. *The Minor League Register.* Durham, N.C.: Baseball America, Inc., 1994.

Leerhsen, Charles. *Crazy Good: The True Story of Dan Patch, the most famous horse in America.* New York: Simon and Schuster, 2008.

MacCambridge, Michael, ed. *ESPN College Football Encyclopedia: the complete history of the game.* New York: ESPN Books, 2005.

Miller, Jeff. *Going Long. The Wild Ten-Year Saga of the Renegade American Football League in the Words of Those Who Lived It.* New York: McGraw-Hill, 2003.

Oberst, Greg and J. Alexander Poulton. *Washington Sports Trivia*. Montreal: Overtime Books, an imprint of Editions de la Montagne Verte, 2010.

O'Neal, Bill. *The American Association: A Baseball History, 1902–1991*. Austin, Texas: Eakin Press, 1991.

Palmer, Pete and Gary Gillete, ed. *The Baseball Encyclopedia*. New York: Barnes and Noble Books, 2004.

Purdy, Dennis. *The Team by Team Encyclopedia of Major League Baseball*. New York: Workman Publishing, 2006.

Reavis, Tracey. *The Nicknames. The Official NBA Encyclopedia (3rd Edition)*. New York: Doubleday, 2000.

Rippel, Joel. *Game of My Life: Minnesota. Memorable Stories of Gophers Football*. Champaign, Ill.: Sports Publishing, LLC, 2007.

Rippel, Joel. *Minnesota Sports Almanac*. St. Paul, Minn.: Minnesota Historical Society Press, 2006.

Rippel, Joel. *75 Memorable Moments in Minnesota Sports*. St. Paul, Minn.: Minnesota Historical Society Press, 2003.

Roberts, Kate. *Minnesota 150. The People, Places and Things That Shape Our State*. St. Paul, Minn.: Minnesota Historical Society Press, 2007.

Sargent, Scott Allen. *The Complete Historical and Reference Guide to the World Hockey Association, 1972–1979*. Tempe, Ariz.: Xaler Press, 1995.

Thornley, Stew, ed. *Minnesotans in Baseball*. Minneapolis: Nodin Press, 2009.

Media Guides/Record Books
Minnesota Timberwolves 2008–09 media guide
Minnesota Vikings 2010 media guide
National Baseball Hall of Fame and Museum 2010 Yearbook
2007–08 Official NBA Guide
2007–08 Official NBA Register
NHL Official Guide and Record Book, 2009–10
University of Minnesota 2010 football media and records book

Other Publications
Crossings, a Stearns County History Museum publication. July 2008.

Websites
www.lpga.com
www.nhl.com
www.pgatour.com
www.profootballhof.com
www.retrosheet.org
http://www.startribune.com/sports/
http://sports.espn.go.com/nfl/news/story?id=3471189
http://sports.espn.go.com/nfl/news/story?id=4409512
http://news.google.com/newspapers?id=i0YaAAAAIBAJ&sjid=2ScEAAAAIBAJ&pg=4400,3522789&dq=minnesota+north+stars&hl=en
http://www.startribune.com/sports/wild/12674787.htm

Joel Rippel

Joel Rippel was born and raised in a small farming town in southern Minnesota. He started working for the weekly newspaper in his hometown when he was 16 and has been working in media ever since. He graduated from the University of Minnesota with a Bachelor of Arts in Journalism and has had six other books published, one of which was a finalist for the Minnesota Book Award. He worked for 17 years at the *Minneapolis Star Tribune* as a news assistant.

J. Alexander Poulton

J. Alexander Poulton is a writer, photographer and genuine sports enthusiast. He's even willing to admit he has "called in sick" during the broadcasts of major sports events so that he can get in as much viewing as possible.

He has earned a BA in English literature and a graduate diploma in journalism, and has over 20 sports books to his credit, including books on hockey, soccer, golf and the Olympics.